Swamp Fox

*General Francis Marion
and his Guerrilla Fighters
of the American Revolutionary War*

by

William Dobein James

Layout and Cover Design Copyright ©2013
All Rights Reserved
Printed in the USA

A SKETCH OF THE LIFE OF BRIG. GEN. FRANCIS MARION
And A History of his Brigade,
From its Rise in June, 1780, until Disbanded in December, 1782;
With Descriptions of Characters and Scenes, not heretofore published.
 Containing also, An Appendix, with Copies of Letters which passed between several of the Leading Characters of that Day; Principally From Gen. Greene to Gen. Marion.
 By William Dobein James, A.M.
During that Period one of Marion's Militia.
At Present one of the Associate Judges in Equity, South Carolina.
 Quae contentio, divina et humana cuncta perniscuit, eoque vecordiae processit uti civilibus studiis bellum finem faceret.—Sall.
 Transcriber's Note on text: Some obvious errors have been corrected. Some spellings are modernized. See notes at end of etext for additional explanations.

 District of South-Carolina.
 —|L. S.|—BE IT REMEMBERED, that on the fifth day of April,———
Anno Domini, one thousand eight hundred and twenty-one, and in the forty-fifth

Table of Contents

Preface..4
Introduction..6

Chapter 1: Early History................................9
Chapter 2: Campaign of 1780............................17
Chapter 3: Campaign of 1781............................48
Chapter 4: Campaign of 1782............................88

Appendix..103

Preface

During the siege of Charleston, in May, 1780, the grammar school at Salem, on Black river, where I had been placed by my father, Major JOHN JAMES, broke up; and I was compelled to abandon my school boy studies, and become a militia man, at the age of fifteen. At that time of life it was a great loss; but still I was so fortunate as to have General MARION as my commander, and my much honoured father, who was a sincere christian, as my adviser and protector. I do not intend to write a history of my own life; but it was thus, that I became in a great measure an eye witness of the scenes hereafter described; and what I did not see, I often heard from others in whom confidence could be placed.

I felt an early inclination to record these events; but Major WEMYSS burnt all my stock of paper, and my little classical library, in my father's house; and, for two years and a half afterwards, I had not the common implements of writing or of reading. This may appear strange at present; but it is a fact, that even our general, when sending out a patrole, would request the officer to try to get him a quire of paper. After the war, other active pursuits prevented me from indulging my inclination; and the public attention, being long fixed upon the bloody wars and great battles in Europe, had lost all relish for our revolutionary history, and its comparatively little conflicts. However, when Dr. RAMSAY announced that he was about to publish his history of South Carolina, I hastily sketched out from memory a short history of MARION'S brigade, for him; which he inserted in fifteen pages of his first volume. This brings it down no lower than the arrival of General GREENE in South Carolina. Fortunately the events of the late war revived the national spirit, and with that a taste for our own history; by it too, my inclination was renewed to communicate that of MARION'S brigade. However, I still wanted materials to confide in more certain than memory.

The last year I happened to mention my wish to Mr. RICHARD SINGELLTON, of Colleton, son-in-law of Major JOHN POSTELL, and he obligingly placed in my hands a bundle of original letters from General MARION to that distinguished officer. Not long after I heard that the late General PETER HORRY had preserved copies of General MARION'S correspondence with General GREENE and other officers; and I applied to his executor, Mr. JAMES GUIGNARD, who very politely placed five duodecimo

Preface

volumes in my hands, closely written by the general. The originals were left by General HORRY with the Rev. M. L. WEEMS, but it appears he made no use of them in his life of MARION. The dates and facts stated in these copies agree pretty well with the account in the history of South Carolina by Dr. RAMSAY, and General MOULTRIE'S memoirs of the American revolution.

I have also taken the pains to consult several of MARION'S officers and men, who still survive. The Hon. THOMAS WATIES gave me considerable information respecting the first part of the general's operations, which I did not witness; as, after MARION'S retreat to the White marsh, I was left sick in North Carolina. During MARION'S struggle with WATSON I had returned, but was confined to my bed with the small pox; and the greater part of that account was received from Captain GAVIN WITHERSPOON, ROBERT WITHERSPOON, Esq. and others. Respecting the affairs about Camden, General CANTEY and Dr. BROWNFIELD gave me much information; and the present sheriff of Charleston district, FRANCIS G. DELIESSELINE, Esq. and myself have compared notes generally on the subject.

Of all these sources of information I have availed myself; besides having recourse to every account of the events of that period which I had it in my power to consult. This, I hope, will account satisfactorily for any departures made from the statement I furnished Dr. RAMSAY.

There are no doubt many errors in my narrative, as nothing human is exempt from them; but it is believed there are not more than usually occur in what is considered accurate history. It may also need correction in other matters, and it may not be pregnant with great events; but still it is a kind of domestic history, which teaches lessons of patience and patriotism, not surpassed in modern, and seldom in ancient times.

William Dobein James

Introduction

The revocation of the edict of Nantz, by Lewis XIV., though highly detrimental to France, proved beneficial to Holland, England and other European countries; which received the protestant refugees, and encouraged their arts and industry. The effects of this unjust and bigoted decree, extended themselves likewise to North America, but more particularly to South Carolina: About seventeen years after its first settlement, in the year 1690, and a short time subsequently, between seventy and eighty French families, fleeing from the bloody persecution excited against them in their mother country, settled on the banks of the Santee. Among these were the ancestors of General FRANCIS MARION. These families extended themselves at first only from the lower ferry at South Santee, in St. James' parish, up to within a few miles of Lenud's ferry, and back from the river into the parish of St. Dennis, called the Orange quarter. From their first settlement, they appear to have conciliated their neighbours, the Sewee and Santee Indians; and to have submitted to their rigorous fate with that resignation and cheerfulness which is characteristic of their nation.—Many must have been the hardships endured by them in settling upon a soil covered with woods, abounding in serpents and beasts of prey, naturally sterile, and infested by a climate the most insalubrious. For a picture of their sufferings read the language of one of them, Judith Manigault, bred a lady in ease and affluence:—"Since leaving France we have experienced every kind of affliction, disease, pestilence, famine, poverty, hard labour; I have been for six months together without tasting bread, working the ground like a slave." They cultivated the barren high lands, and at first naturally attempted to raise wheat, barley and other European grains upon them, until better taught by the Indians. Tradition informs us, that men and their wives worked together in felling trees, building houses, making fences, and grubbing up their grounds, until their settlements were formed; and afterwards continued their labours at the whip-saw,[1] and in burning tar for market. Such was their industry, that in fourteen years after their first settlement, and according to the first certain account of them, they were in prosperous circumstances. In the year 1701, John Lawson, then Surveyor General of the province, visited these enterprising people, and as there are but two copies of his "Journal of a thousand miles travelled through several nations of Indians", known at present to be in

Introduction

existence, no apology appears to be necessary for presenting extracts of the most interesting parts of it to the reader:—

"On December 28th, 1700, I began my voyage for North Carolina, from Charleston, in a large canoe. At four in the afternoon, at half flood, we passed over the breach through the marsh, leaving Sullivan's Island on our starboard; the first place we designed for was Santee river, on which there is a colony of French protestants, allowed and encouraged by the lords proprietors."—After passing through Sewee bay and up Santee, the mouth of which was fresh, he visited the Sewees; "formerly," he says, "a large nation, though now very much decreased, since the English have seated their lands, and all other nations of Indians are observed to partake of the same fate. With hard rowing we got that night (11th January, 1701,) to Mons. Eugee's[2] house, which stands about fifteen miles up the river, being the first christian dwelling we met withal in that settlement, and were very courteously received by him and his wife. Many of the French follow a trade with the Indians, living very conveniently for that interest. Here are about seventy families seated on this river, who live as decently and happily as any planters in these southward parts of America. The French being a temperate, industrious people, some of them bringing very little effects, yet by their endeavours and mutual assistance among themselves (which is highly commendable) have outstript our English, who brought with them larger fortunes. We lay all that night at Mons. Eugee's,[2] and the next morning set out further to go the remainder of our voyage by land. At noon we came up with several French plantations, meeting with several creeks by the way: the French were very officious in assisting with their small dories, to pass over these waters, (whom we met coming from their church) being all of them very clean and decent in their apparel—their houses and plantations suitable in neatness and contrivance. They are all of the same opinion with the church of Geneva. Towards the afternoon we came to Mons. L'Jandro's,[3] where we got our dinner. We got that night to Mons. Galliar's,[4] who lives in a very curious contrived house, built of brick and stone, which is gotten near that place. Near here, comes in the road from Charleston and the rest of the English settlement, it being a very good way by land and not above thirty-six miles."[5] After this, our author gives a long description of his difficulty and danger in crossing the Santee in a small canoe, in time of a freshet. He then goes on as follows:—"We intended for Mons. Galliar's jun. but were lost. When we got to the house we found several of the French inhabitants, who treated us very courteously; wondering about our undertaking such a voyage through a country inhabited by none but savages, and them of so different nations and tongues. After we had refreshed ourselves, we parted from a very kind, loving, affable people, who wished us a safe and prosperous voyage." Our traveller had now arrived at the extreme boundary of the white population of South Carolina, and consequently of the United States, and this was but forty miles from Charleston. In the course of one hundred and twenty years what a change, and what a subject for reflection! But, to return to the French refugees. The same persevering industry and courteous manners which distinguished the ancestors, were handed down to their children, and are still conspicuous among their descendants of the third and fourth generations. Most of them may be classed among our useful and honourable citizens, and many have highly distinguished themselves in the state, both in civil and military affairs: but in the latter character, the subject of these memoirs, General FRANCIS MARION, stands forth the most prominent and illustrious example.[6]

Footnotes

1. Gen. Horry states, that his grandfather and grandmother commenced the handsome fortune they left, by working together at the whip-saw.

2. Huger, who lived in the fork between South Santee and Wambaw Creek.

3. Gendron.

4. Gaillard's.

5. Near this place the French laid out a town, and called it Jamestown; whence the name St. James', Santee.

6. After leaving the house of Bartholomew Gaillard, jun. on the east side of Santee, Mr. Lawson saw no more settlements of the whites. He visited the Santee Indians, who, from his description of the country, must have lived about Nelson's ferry and Scott's lake. In passing up the river, the Indian path led over a hill, where he saw, as he says, "the most amazing prospect I had seen since I had been in Carolina. We travelled by a swamp side, which swamp, I believe to be no less than twenty miles over; the other side being, as far as I could well discern; there appearing great ridges of mountains bearing from us W.N.W. One Alp, with a top like a sugar loaf, advanced its head above the rest very considerably; the day was very serene, which gave us the advantage of seeing a long way; these mountains were clothed all over with trees, which seemed to us to be very large timbers. At the sight of this fair prospect we stayed all night; our Indian going before half an hour, provided three fat turkeys e'er we got up to him." The prospect he describes is evidently the one seen from the Santee Hills; the old Indian path passed over a point of one of these at Captain Baker's plantation, from which the prospect extends more than twenty miles; and the Alp, which was so conspicuous, must have been Cook's Mount, opposite Stateburgh.—Our traveller afterwards visited the Congaree, the Wateree, and Waxhaw Indians, in South Carolina, and divers tribes in North Carolina, as far as Roanoke; and it is melancholy to think, that all of these appear to be now extinct. They treated him with their best; such as bear meat and oil, venison, turkeys, maize, cow peas, chinquepins, hickory nuts and acorns. The Kings and Queens of the different tribes always took charge of him as their guest.

Chapter 1:
Early History

Francis Marion was born at Winyaw, near Georgetown, South Carolina, in the year 1732;—memorable for giving birth to many distinguished American patriots. Marion was of French extraction; his grandfather, Gabriel, left France soon after the revocation of the edict of Nantz, in 1685, on account of his being a protestant, and retired from persecution to this new world, then a wilderness; no doubt under many distresses and dangers, and with few of the facilities with which emigrants settle new, but rich countries, at the present day. His son, also called Gabriel, was the father of five sons, Isaac, Gabriel, Benjamin, Francis, and Job, and of two daughters, grandmothers of the families of the Mitchells, of Georgetown, and of the Dwights, formerly of the same place, but now of St. Stephen's parish.

Of the education of FRANCIS MARION, we have no account; but from the internal evidence afforded by his original letters, it appears to have been no more than a plain English one; for the Huguenots seem to have already so far assimilated themselves to the country as to have forgotten their French. It was indeed a rare thing, in this early state of our country, to receive any more than the rudiments of an English education; since men were too much employed in the clearing and tilth of barren lands, to attend much to science.

Such an education seemed to dispose Marion to be modest and reserved in conversation; to think, if not to read much; and, above all, not to be communicative. An early friend of his, the late Captain John Palmer, has stated, that his first inclination was for a seafaring life, and that at the age of sixteen he made a voyage to the West Indies. The vessel in which he embarked foundered at sea, and the crew, consisting of six persons, took to an open boat, without water or provisions: but, providentially, a dog swam to them from the ship, whose blood served them for drink, and his raw flesh for food, for six days; on the seventh, Francis Marion, and three of the crew, reached land, but the other two perished at sea. Things which appear accidental at the time, often sway the destinies of human life. Thus it was, that from the effect of this narrow escape, and the entreaties of a tender mother, Francis Marion was induced to abandon the sea, for an element, on which he was to become singularly useful. His mother's maiden name was Cordes, and she also was of French extraction. Engaged in cultivating the soil, we hear no more of Marion for ten years. Mr. Henry Ravenel, of Pineville, now more than 70 years of age, knew him in the year 1758; he had then lost his father; and, removing with his mother and brother Gabriel from Georgetown, they settled for one year near Frierson's lock, on the present Santee canal. The next year Gabriel removed to Belle Isle, in St. Stephen's parish, late the residence of his son, the Hon. Robert Marion. Francis settled himself in St. John's, at a place called Pond Bluff, from the circumstance of there being a pond at the bottom of a bluff, fronting the river low grounds. This place is situated about four miles below Eutaw, on the Santee; and he continued to hold it during life.[1] Others fix his settling in St. John's, at a later period: this is of little consequence, but what is of some, was that in this most useful of all stations, a tiller of the ground, he was industrious and successful. In the same year, 1759, the Cherokee war broke out, and he turned out as a volunteer, in his brother's troop of provincial cavalry. In 1761, he served in the expedition under Col. Grant, as a lieutenant in Captain Wm. Moultrie's company, forming part of a provincial regiment, commanded by Col. Middleton. It is believed that he distinguished himself in this expedition, in a severe conflict between Col. Grant and the Indians, near Etchoee, an Indian town; but, if he did so, the particulars have not been handed down to us, by any official account. General Moultrie says of him, "he was an active, brave, and hardy soldier; and an excellent partisan officer." We come now to that part of Marion's life, where, acting in a more conspicuous situation, things are known of him, with more certainty. In the beginning of the year 1775, he was elected one, of what was then called the provincial congress of South Carolina, from St. John's. This was the public body which agreed to the famous continental association, recommended by congress, to prevent the importation of goods, wares, and merchandizes, from Great Britain: they likewise put a stop to all suits at law, except where debtors refused to renew their obligations, and to give reasonable security, or when justly suspected of intentions to leave the province, or to defraud their creditors; and they appointed committees in the several districts and parishes in the state, which were called committees of public safety, to carry these acts into effect. These exercised high municipal authority, and supported generally by a population sometimes intemperate, inflicted singular punishments[2] upon such as were not only guilty, but even suspected, of infringing the association. The provincial congress also, after receiving the news of the battle of Lexington, determined upon a defensive war, and resolved to raise two regiments of infantry, and one of cavalry. Marion was elected a captain in the second regiment of these two, of which William Moultrie was colonel. Charles Cotesworth Pinckney, and Thomas Pinckney, since so much distinguished, were likewise elected captains in this regiment at the same time. The first of Captain Marion's appearing in arms against the British, was in the latter part of this year, when he acted as one of three captains under Colonel Motte, in taking possession of Fort Johnson, on James Island. On this occasion much resistance was expected,

Chapter 1: Early History

but the garrison abandoned the fort, and escaped to two British vessels, the Tamar and Cherokee, then lying in Charleston harbour. In the autumn of the same year a post was established at Dorchester, where it was thought prudent to send part of the military stores, and the public records out of Charleston; and here Captain Marion had the command. This is only worthy of remark in the circumstance, that as the climate of this place is remarkably bad in autumn, it shows that our patriots had already so much enthusiasm in the cause in which they had embarked, that they refused no station, however perilous. As the provincial congress and committees of public safety exercised all the legislative and judicial powers in the state, as might have been expected, they soon became too complicated for them, and were thrown into great confusion. The criminal code was still left in force; but there were no judges to exercise that jurisdiction. The provincial congress, therefore, without waiting for a convention of the people, framed a constitution: by this they took the name of the general assembly of South Carolina, and limited their own continuance until the 21st October, 1776; and, in every two years after that period, a general election was to take place for members of the assembly. The legislative powers were vested in a president, the assembly, and a legislative council, to be chosen out of their own body. All resolutions of the continental and provincial congress, and all laws then of force, were continued. They passed a law, that only two thirds of the rice made in the state should be permitted to be exported, the other third was to remain in the country for its consumption, and for exchange for the necessary articles of life: and upon these prices were to be fixed; it was recommended to the people to cultivate cotton; the breed of sheep was directed to be improved; and, after a certain day, none were to be killed for market or home consumption; but the continental congress soon after, passed a law that no rice should be exported; and it was submitted to, without a murmur. A vice-president and privy council of six members were elected, and among other duties, were to exercise chancery jurisdiction; and other judges were directed to be chosen by the general assembly.

In a few years, such confusion followed, that we shall see the president, soon after denominated governor, and two of the privy council, exercising all the civil and military powers of the state.

John Rutledge was chosen president, Henry Laurens vice-president, and ex-officio president of the privy council. In this year, (1776,) Francis Marion had risen to the rank of major in the second regiment, and was stationed with his colonel in the fort at Sullivan's Island. He was in the action of the 28th of June, between that fort and nine of the British ships, under Sir Peter Parker. Of the particulars of this battle, every one has heard, and they need not be narrated here. Two of the ships carried fifty guns, the ship Bristol, commodore Sir Peter Parker, and the Experiment; and as powder was very scarce in the fort, the orders were, "mind the commodore!" "Fire at the two fifty gun ships." Col.

Moultrie received the thanks of the commander in chief, of congress, Gen. Lee, and of president Rutledge, for his gallant conduct in that victory; and, what was more, the heart-felt gratitude of his countrymen. The fort was called by his name, and he was raised to the rank of brigadier general. His major then rose to the rank of lieut. colonel. This action excited the highest resentment in the breasts of the British rulers; and in the end they inflicted severe vengeance on the state of South Carolina. Three years, however, elapsed before they made another attempt. In December, 1778, a British fleet of thirty seven sail, arrived off Savannah in Georgia, and landed about 4000 men. One half of these, under Col. Campbell, immediately made an attack upon the town. Gen. Howe, with six or seven hundred Americans, attempted to oppose them; but was defeated at the first onset. The enemy took possession of the town; and, as the Georgia militia were backward in turning out, the whole country soon fell under their dominion. Shortly after the taking of Savannah, Gen. Lincoln took command of the American army, and Gen. Prevost of the British. On the 3d of Feb. 1779, Gen. Moultrie, with a party of about 300 militia, mostly citizens of Charleston and Beaufort, with the company of ancient artillery of Charleston, was posted at Beaufort, where he heard the enemy was advancing. He immediately dispatched his aid, Capt. Francis Kinloch, to reconnoitre; while he moved forward on the road to Beaufort ferry. Kinloch returning soon, stated the supposed force of the British, and that they were near upon the road; Moultrie now pushed on to gain a defile, but found it occupied by the enemy. There being no alternative, he then drew up his men in open ground, with two field pieces in the centre, and one on the right. The British force was two companies of picked light infantry, posted under cover of a swamp. The militia engaged them, and fought under this disadvantage till their ammunition was all expended, and Moultrie ordered a retreat; but the British made a simultaneous movement, and it became a drawn battle. Lieut. Wilkins of the ancient artillery, was mortally wounded, and seven men were killed. Capt. Heyward, Lieuts. Sawyer and Brown, and fifteen men, were wounded. In the general's account of the action, the loss of the British is not stated; he speaks highly of the conduct of his officers and men; particularly of Capt. John Barnwell; and indeed it was no little matter, thus to bring militia, in the open field, to fight regulars under cover.

    Lincoln's force was fluctuating, as it consisted principally of militia, who could not be brought under control; and in the midst of arms, when the enemy were at the distance of only three miles, their officers refused to subject them to the articles of war; and insisted upon their being tried by the militia laws of the state, which only subjected them to a small pecuniary fine. The case too was a flagrant one; a private of Col. Kershaw's regiment had absented himself from guard, and upon being reproved by his captain, gave him abusive language; the captain ordered him under guard, and the man attempted

Chapter 1: Early History

to shoot his officer; but was prevented. This case was referred to the general assembly then sitting, who also refused to bring the militia under the articles of war. Had Gen. Jackson lately submitted to such an interference with his authority, we should never have heard of the glorious victory of New Orleans. Gen. Lincoln would have nothing more to do with the militia, and gave up the command of them to Gen. Moultrie, to act with them as a separate corps. Pursuant to this resolution, and after calling a council of war, he marched off (20th April) about 2000 light troops and cavalry, for Augusta, leaving his baggage to follow. Near Augusta, he expected a reinforcement of 3000 men, and his intentions were to take possession of some strong post in Georgia, to circumscribe the limits of the enemy, and to prevent their receiving recruits from the Cherokee Indians, and tories. He left Gen. Moultrie, with about 1200 militia, at Black Swamp. As soon as Gen. Prevost heard of this movement, he availed himself of it, and immediately crossed over the Savannah, from Abercorn to Purysburgh, twenty-five miles below Black Swamp, with the intention of surprising Moultrie, but he, receiving intelligence of his crossing, retired to Coosawhatchie. At this place he left a rear guard, and pitched his head quarters on the hill to the eastward of Tulifinny, two miles in advance towards Charleston. (1st May.) After reconnoitring the fords of Coosawhatchie, and Tulifinny above the bridges, the general found so little water in the swamps, from the excessive drought which then prevailed,[3] that he determined not to risk an action at this post. He was about to send one of his aids to bring off his rear guard, when Col. John Laurens offered himself as a volunteer for that service; he was readily accepted, and captain, afterwards Major John James, with 150 picked riflemen, was sent to cover his flanks: these, with the rear guard, made near a fourth of the retreating army. Instead of bringing off the rear guard, Col. Laurens drew them over to the east side of the river, posted the riflemen at the bridge, threw off the planks, and engaged the enemy. The British occupied the houses on the west bank, from which they kept up a galling fire; a number of Laurens' men were killed and wounded, and, as he was very conspicuous on horse back in regimentals, with a large white plume, he was soon wounded himself, and his horse killed. Laurens then retired, and captain, afterwards Col. Shubrick, ordered a retreat. In the mean time Moultrie had decamped, and the riflemen were obliged, as the planks were thrown off, to pass Tulifinny and Pocotaligo bridges on the string pieces; and did not overtake the main body till they had passed Saltketcher bridge. Here let us pause for a moment, and take a view of the ground; twelve miles of country had been passed over in one morning, which was a continued defile of causeway, lined on both sides with either thick woods, or ditches and fences, and four rivers had been crossed; over which were high bridges, and only a slight skirmish had taken place. True, the swamps above the bridges were dry, but then they were so wide and thick, that the British would never have ventured into them.

It is likewise true that Col. Laurens said the militia would not fight, yet the riflemen stood till they were ordered to retreat, and their retreat had like to have been cut off. Laurens was not wrong in fighting, for it is always best to keep militia employed: but in engaging without orders, and in not burning down the houses near the river, he is blamed by Gen. Moultrie.[4] However Moultrie himself was more to blame in suffering the enemy to pass over Coosawhatchie. At least they ought not to have been permitted to cross the Saltketcher. There is no doubt but Moultrie was a firm patriot and a brave soldier, but he acted now under the impulse of an opinion, which then generally prevailed among the officers of the South Carolina troops, that Charleston was all important, and if taken, the state must be lost. We shall see the effect of this system in the end. In the same manner the Edisto and Ashley were now passed, without striking a blow. The Americans suffered greatly both for provisions and for the want of water, drinking out of every puddle in the road, however filthy. The enemy, on the contrary, passed through the richest part of the state, and were suffered to scatter themselves abroad, and to satiate themselves with choice fare, and valuable plunder. General Moultrie continued his march to Charleston, and Prevost took post before the lines.

We have for some time lost sight of Lieut. Col. Marion, and the reader may naturally inquire, was he at Tulifinny? He was not. With the second regiment under his command, he was in garrison at fort Moultrie. Before Gen. Moultrie broke up his camp at Black Swamp, he wrote to Gen. Lincoln to give him advice of the movement of the enemy to Purysburgh, and from time to time of their progress to Charleston; but Lincoln marched up to Augusta, crossed over into Georgia, and moved down on the other side of the river for some time, very deliberately.[5] However, from Jannett's ferry, he writes a letter, of which the following is an extract: "If the enemy should give public evidence of their designs against Charleston, I think, with your force, as you are in possession of strong passes, you will be able to stop their progress and give us time to come up." On the 10th of May, he again writes to Gen. Moultrie, "We are making, and shall continue to make, every exertion for the relief of Charleston. The baggage will be left. The inability of the men only, will put a period to our daily marches. Our men are full of spirits. Do not give up, or suffer the people to despair." But the governor and council did despair already, for a majority of them had finally offered to capitulate, and proposed a neutrality, during the war between Great Britain and South Carolina; and the question, whether the state should belong to Great Britain, or remain one of the United States, to be determined by the treaty of peace; from this offer, Gen. Gadsden and Mr. Thomas Ferguson dissented. To carry terms so disgraceful, to Prevost, Col. Laurens was pitched upon; but he indignantly refused to be the bearer. Cols. M'Intosh and Roger Smith were then persuaded to go with a flag. The British commander appointed Col. Prevost, as commissioner to receive them; and

Chapter 1: Early History

he delivered a message from the general, "that he had nothing to do with the governor, that his business was with Gen. Moultrie; and as the garrison was in arms, they must surrender prisoners of war." At this answer, the governor and council looked blank; and some were for submitting even to this degrading proposal: but Moultrie cut the conference short, by declaring, "that as it was left to him, he would fight to the last extremity." Laurens, who was present, and sitting, bounded to his feet at the expression, raised his hands, and thanked his God! Thus it was only by a mistake of Prevost, as to the high powers of the civil authority, that the town, and the state of South Carolina, were then saved. What renders this offer the more astonishing, was, that the garrison, 3180 strong, were in good spirits, and an army under Lincoln, was marching to their assistance, on the rear of the enemy; who were not much stronger than the besieged, being computed at 3680 men.[6] Early the next morning, Prevost decamped, and retreated to John's and James Islands. (May 13th.) There was great rejoicing in the town; but the consequence to which it had arrived, by repelling two attempts of the enemy, only brought against it a greater armament, and in the end, sunk it into deeper distress. An attack upon the British at Stono ferry, was now planned by Gen. Lincoln. Gen. Moultrie, was to throw over on James Island, all the troops which could be spared from the town, and make a feint on that side, or attack, if a favourable opportunity offered; while the principal effort was to be made by Lincoln, at Stono. He made the attack before Moultrie could cooperate, (June 20) and the enemy remaining in their lines, and being reinforced, obliged him to retreat. In this affair a few men were killed, and Col. Roberts, of the artillery, mortally wounded. His loss was greatly and justly lamented. William Richardson Davie, lately deceased, and afterwards so much celebrated as Gen. Davie, was among the wounded. Prevost, soon after this, retreated along the chain of islands on the coast, until he reached Port Royal and Savannah. During the time Prevost lay before the lines of Charleston, Maj. Benjamin Huger, an active officer, a wise statesman, and a virtuous citizen, was unfortunately killed. What rendered his fate the more melancholy, was, that the act was done by the mistake of his own countrymen. It was at this time also, that Gen. Count Pulaski, a Polander, began to distinguish himself as a partisan. His address in single combat, was greatly celebrated. Col. Kowatch, under his command, was killed before the lines, and shamefully mutilated by the British. Of the campaign of 1779, it was not the intention of the author to give a minute detail; but only to sketch out those feelings, and that line of conduct, in the cabinet and field, which, followed up in the succeeding year, brought ruin and disgrace upon the country.

Footnotes

1. *Pond Bluff is presently at the bottom of Lake Marion*
2. *Such as tarring and feathering.*
3. *The fine spring at Tulifinny had then entirely failed.*
4. *Volume Moultrie's memoirs, p. 403-4.*
5. *Lincoln's letter, 20th April.*
6. *1st vol. Moultrie's memoirs, from p. 425 to 435.*

Chapter 2:
Campaign of 1780

Sir Henry Clinton arrives with an army of 12,000 men in South Carolina. The General Assembly sitting in Charleston, break up. Gen. Lincoln shuts himself up in the town, and Clinton lays siege to it. Before the town is entirely hemmed in, Marion dislocates his ankle, and retires into the country. The town capitulates. Tarleton's career of slaughter. Defeat of Gen. Huger at Monk's Corner and of Buford at the Waxhaws. Rising of the people in Williamsburgh, and at Pedee. Gen. Marion sent to them as a commander. Gates, defeat. Marion retakes 150 American prisoners at Nelson's Ferry. Maj. Wemyss sent against him; he retreats to the White Marsh, in North Carolina. Returns and defeats the tories at Black Mingo and the fork of Black river. Attempt on Georgetown frustrated. Marion takes post at Snow Island. Sumter's career. Ferguson's defeat. Spirit of the whigs begins to revive.

The year 1780, was the most eventful one, in the annals of South Carolina. The late failure of the attack on Savannah; the little opposition which Gen. Prevost met with, in a march of more than one hundred miles through the state; the conduct of the planters, in submitting, to save their property; and the well known weakness of the southern army; all conspired to induce the enemy to believe, that Charleston, and South Carolina, would become an easy prey. Sir Henry Clinton, their commander in chief, meditating a formidable expedition against them; with this view sailed from New York on the 26th December, 1779, with an army, which, with subsequent reinforcements amounted to about 12,000 men. To oppose this great force, Gen. Lincoln had not more than two thousand, a great part of which was militia. His head quarters were in Charleston, where the general assembly were setting in calm deliberation, for they had not yet heard of the rising storm. Lieut. Col. Marion, had command of the out-post of this little army, at Sheldon, near Pocotaligo, where he had orders to watch the motions of Prevost, and prevent him from obtaining supplies of provisions, from the Carolina side of Savannah river. It was expected he was to remain here for some time, and great confidence was reposed in him, by Gen. Lincoln, as appears by his letters, at this period. The British had a tedious passage, in which they lost part of their ordnance, most of their artillery, and all the horses, destined to mount their cavalry. On the 11th Feb. 1780, they landed about thirty miles from Charleston. The assembly sitting there, immediately broke up, after delegating, "till ten days after their next session, to John Rutledge, and such of his council as he could conveniently consult, a power to do every thing necessary for the public good; except the taking away the life of a citizen, without a legal trial." This was nearly the same power, with which the senate of Rome, invested their dictators. But a resolution, fatal in its consequences, was unanimously adopted by this assembly: namely, to defend the town to the utmost extremity. The power, thus delegated to the governor and council, was carried into effect afterwards, with vigour, and with what would now be thought an infraction of private rights. But in the spirit of the times, and the public situation, such vigour was necessary. The governor's council, was composed of upright and virtuous men, and John Rutledge was one of the most distinguished sons, to whom South Carolina has given birth. His eloquence was proverbial, both in congress, and at home. It was that of Demosthenes, concise, energetic, and commanding. There was something in his very manner, and the tone of his voice, that riveted the attention of his audience. They stood subdued before him. He swayed the councils of the state, he swayed the councils of the general who commanded the southern army: and if he erred, he erred with a good conscience, and from the purest motives.

The first order issued by Governor Rutledge, was, to call out the drafted militia, for the defence of the town, under pain of confiscation of property. This order was but partially obeyed;—the militia, who were friendly to the cause, had been much harassed in the last campaign, and it was generally known that the small-pox was in the town. At the same time, the governor sent out many influential officers, to secure the execution of his first order; and though intended only to operate for the present, this last order was in time productive of a fortunate result; as these officers afterwards headed the people. In the mean time, Gen. Lincoln had ordered Lieut. Col. Marion to select two hundred men, out of the three regiments with him, at Sheldon, and to march immediately to town. (31st Jan.) No troops were to be left in the field but two hundred light infantry, and the horse under Col. Washington. Marion repaired to town, according to orders; but before the garrison was hemmed in by the enemy, he, by accident, in attempting to escape from a drinking party, dislocated his ankle. Gen. Lincoln had issued an order, "that all supernumerary officers, and all officers who were unfit for duty, must quit the garrison, and retire into the country." In consequence of this order, Marion retired to St. John's. He was afterwards obliged to move about, from house to house, as favoured by friends, and often to hide in the woods, until he got better; but, as soon as he was able, he collected a few friends, and joined Gen. De Kalb, who was then advancing, with about fourteen hundred men, of the Maryland and Delaware troops, towards South Carolina. The correspondence of Gen. Horry here breaks off suddenly; and we hear no more of Marion for five months. But an accident, which must have appeared to him a great misfortune, at the

Chapter 2: Campaign of 1780

time, was afterwards productive of the most happy effects. Another has been noted only a few pages back.

In the mean time, the enemy proceeded cautiously in the siege of Charleston. They formed a depot on James Island, and erected a fortification on it, and the main, near Wappoo cut. On the 28th of March they crossed Ashley river, near the ferry, and made a lodgement in Charleston neck. Col. Laurens, with the light infantry, skirmished with them; but, as they greatly exceeded him in numbers, he was obliged to retire within the lines. On the night of the 1st of April, Sir Henry Clinton commenced his first parallel, at the distance of eleven hundred yards from the American works. On the 7th, twelve sail of the enemy's ships passed Fort Moultrie, under a heavy fire. The garrison had been assiduous in preparing for defence; the old works were strengthened, and lines and redoubts were extended from Ashley to Cooper river. A strong abbatis was made in front, and a deep, wet ditch was opened from the marsh on one side, to that on the other, and the lines were so constructed as to rake it. On the 10th, the enemy had completed their first parallel, and Gen. Lincoln was summoned to surrender; but refused. All attempts at removing the force besieged, out of the town, had, while it was practicable, been opposed by the governor and council, and the officers of the South Carolina troops; and Gen. Lincoln, had not the resolution to counteract them. At length it was thought advisable, that the governor and three of his council should leave the town; and that Lieut. Gov. Gadsden and five others should remain. The ships of war, in the harbour of Charleston, being quite inadequate to oppose the force which had passed Fort Moultrie, were divested of their guns, to reinforce the batteries, and were sunk nearly opposite the exchange, to impede the passage of the enemy up Cooper river. Soon after this, Sir Henry Clinton, being reinforced by two thousand five hundred men, under Lord Cornwallis, pushed them over Cooper river, and enclosed the besieged on the side of St. Thomas' parish and Christ church; and the town was now completely invested by land and water. About this time, the American forces in the field having been defeated, as hereafter to be narrated, and the British having completed their second parallel, an offer to capitulate was made by Lincoln, to Sir Henry Clinton, and rejected. The batteries of the besiegers, having now obtained a decided superiority over those of the besieged, when the third parallel had opened its cannonade, and the British having crossed the wet ditch by sap, they opened a fire of rifles within twenty-five yards of the Americans. The caution of Sir Henry Clinton, in advancing so slowly, had been extreme, and the unsuspecting security of the Americans was still great; but Gen. Duportail, a French officer of engineers, having arrived in town before the communication was closed with the country, declared, that the works of the besieged were not tenable, and might have been stormed ten days before. This disclosed his true situation, and induced Gen. Lincoln to listen to a capitulation, which was proposed to him on the 8th of May. From that until the 10th, the negociation was continued. On the 11th, the capitulation was agreed to, and, on the next day, the Americans marched out and grounded their arms. After a siege of a month and fourteen days, 2500 men submitted to an army of 12,000; and it was only surprising they held out so long. The continental troops and sailors were to remain prisoners of war until exchanged; the militia were permitted to return home as prisoners on parole, which, as long as they observed it, should secure them from being molested in their property.

On the morning, when the Americans had paraded to surrender, tears were seen coursing down the cheeks of Gen. Moultrie.

The loss of the Americans, in the siege, was not great; only five officers of distinction: Col. Parker, and Capts. Bowman, Moultrie, Templeton and Neyle, were killed. During the siege, Gen. Lincoln called two councils of war, to devise the means of retreating from the town, but all attempts of that kind were opposed, first by the civil authority, next by the South Carolina officers, and finally by the inhabitants. He ought not to have entered the town; he had the example of the illustrious Washington before him, who had declined to act in that manner, and had thus preserved the independence of his country. The American army acting in the country, would have kept up the spirits of the militia, and kept the British from mounting their cavalry, and gaining supplies of provisions, with such ease as they did. Although Lincoln's force was small, it was at least equal to that of Gen. Washington, when he retreated over the Delaware, in 1776. The country was not so open, and more fit for a partisan warfare, than New Jersey, and in a few months the climate would have fought his battles. It was not intended by the author to narrate the particulars of the siege of Charleston; these have been detailed by the enlightened historian of South Carolina, Dr. Ramsay. But the effects of it upon the minds of the people in the country, come more particularly within his province; since they would hereafter be disposed to act according as they were affected, by passing incidents. There being now no force in the field, but the two hundred light infantry, under Gen. Huger, and the horse under Col. Washington; which were those mentioned in Lincoln's order to Gen. Marion; the British were suffered to detach small parties through the country, and to take all the horses which were fit, either to transport their cannon and baggage, or to mount their cavalry. In one month after their landing, Col. Tarleton had his legion mounted, and began his career of slaughter. On the 18th March, he surprised a party of 80 militia, at Saltketcher bridge, killed and wounded several, and dispersed the rest. On the 23d, he put to flight another party at Ponpon, killed three, wounded one, and took four prisoners. On the 27th, near Rantowle's bridge, he had a rencounter with Col. Washington, at the head of his legion of 300 men; Tarleton was worsted in this affair, and lost seven men, prisoners. On the 13th April, the American infantry and cavalry under Gen. Huger, lay, the infantry at Biggen church, and the cavalry under Col. Washington, at Monk's corner. Col. Tarleton with Ferguson's corps of marksmen, advanced on from the quarter-house to Goose Creek, where he was joined by Col. Webster, with the 33d and 64th regiments of infantry. There an attack upon the American post was concerted, and it was judged advisable to make it in the night, as that would render the superiority of Washington's cavalry useless. A servant of one of Huger's officers was taken on the road, and he agreed for a few dollars, to conduct the enemy through a by-road, to Monk's corner. At three o'clock in the morning, they charged Washington's guard on the main road, and pursued them into the camp. The Americans were completely surprised. Major Vernier, of Pulaski's legion, and twenty-five men, were killed. One hundred officers, and dragoons, fifty waggons loaded with ammunition, clothing and arms, and four hundred horses, with their accoutrements, were taken. A most valuable acquisition to the British. Major Cochrane with the British legion of infantry, forced the passage at Biggen bridge, and drove Gen. Huger and the infantry before him.—In this affair, Major James Conyers, of the Americans, distinguished himself by a skilful retreat, and by calling off the attention of the enemy from his sleeping friends, to himself. The British had only one officer and two men wounded. The account of the loss of the Americans in this affair, is taken from Tarleton, who blames "the injudicious conduct of the American commander, who besides making a false disposition of his corps, by placing his cavalry in front of the bridge, during the night, and his infantry in the rear, neglected sending patroles in front of his videttes." In this surprise, the British made free use of the bayonet, the houses in Monk's corner, then a village, were afterwards deserted, and long bore the marks of deadly thrust, and much bloodshed. Col. White soon after took the command of the American cavalry, but with no better fortune. On the 5th May, he took a British officer and seventeen men of the legion, at Ball's plantation, near Strawberry, in the morning, and pushed back twenty-five miles, to Lenud's ferry, on Santee. While crossing there, Tarleton surprised him, at three in the afternoon; who states, that five officers and 36 men of the Americans were killed and wounded, and seven officers and sixty dragoons were taken; while he lost only two men, and retook his dragoons. Cols. White and Washington, Major Jamieson, and several officers and men, escaped by swimming the river, but many perished in the like attempt.[1] Thus the American corps of cavalry and infantry, in the open field, was completely annihilated, and from the Saltketcher to the Santee, a distance of one hundred and twenty miles, either terror or a general depression of spirits, had spread through the country. What served to increase this, was the cannonade at the town. This was a novel thing in South Carolina, and along water courses, it was heard more than one hundred miles. In that distance, there were but few families, who had not a husband, father, brother or son in the garrison; and these listened to the sound, with the deepest anxiety, and, as was natural, with no little despondency.

As soon as the town had surrendered, Lord Cornwallis, with 2500 men, and five field pieces, marched from St. Thomas' to Nelson's ferry. Thence he detached Tarleton, with 700 infantry and cavalry, in quest of Gen. Caswell and Col. Buford, who had been approaching to the relief of Charleston, with about 700 militia, and between 3 and 400 continentals. At Camden, Caswell, with the militia, quitted Buford, who then commanded the continentals, and retreated by the way of Pedee. Buford's regiment was soon after placed under the command of Gen. Huger, as an escort to Gov. Rutledge, then at Camden; and was detained, with a fatal security, by the general, for two days in that place. And so much off their guard, were our rulers themselves, that Gov. Rutledge, and his council, were soon after hospitably entertained, at Clermont, by Col. Rugely, an Englishman, professedly opposed to the American cause. At midnight, he woke them up, advised them of Tarleton's approach, and with some difficulty, persuaded them to escape; at daylight, Tarleton arrived at Clermont. That morning, Huger gave up the command again to Buford, and took the Charlotte road, with the governor and his two remaining council, Daniel Huger and John L. Gervais. Buford proceeded on rapidly, upon the Salisbury road, and from circumstances, his baggage waggons must have been sent on before he took the command again, that morning; otherwise, in making the very quick march he did, they must have been left far in his rear. But Tarleton blames him, for sending them ahead, because they might have served him as a rampart, and other historians have adopted his account. After a pursuit of one hundred miles, in fifty-four hours, Tarleton approached Buford, about forty miles from Camden, and twenty-six from Clermont; and dispatched Capt. David Kinloch with a flag, summoning him to surrender upon the terms granted to the garrison of Charleston. Buford called a council of his officers, who deeming it a deception, he continued his march. In the afternoon, Tarleton overtook him, unfortunately, in an open wood, and cut to pieces his rear guard. At the sound of his bugle, Buford drew up his men, all infantry; but Capt. Carter, (not Benjamin,) who commanded his artillery, and led the van, continued his march. Tarleton advanced, with his infantry in the centre, and his cavalry on the wings. He was checked by Buford's fire; but the cavalry wheeling, gained his rear. Seeing no hope of any longer making a defence, Buford sent Ensign Cruitt with a flag of truce, and grounded his arms. Disregarding the flag, and the rules of civilized warfare, Tarleton cut Cruitt down, and charged upon Buford, with his cavalry in the rear; while Maj. Cochrane, an infuriated Scotchman, rushed with fixed bayonets, in front. A few of Buford's men, resumed their arms, and fired, when the British were within ten steps, but with little effect;[2] as might have been expected, from what has been stated.

Chapter 2: Campaign of 1780

Buford's regiment was entirely broken by the charge, no quarters were given by the British; 113 men were killed of the Americans, and 151 so badly wounded as to be left on the ground. This was nearly two thirds of the whole American force, according to Tarleton's own account; and the manner in which those left on the ground were mangled, is told, by others, as horrible. No habitation was near, but the lone cabin of a poor widow woman; and the situation of the dead, was fortunate, when compared with that of the living. Tarleton says, he lost but two officers, and three privates killed, and one officer and thirteen privates wounded. The massacre took place at the spot where the road from Lancaster to Chesterfield now crosses the Salisbury road. The news of these two events, the surrender of the town, and the defeat of Buford, were spread through the country about the same time, and the spirit of the whigs, sunk into despondency. The American cause appeared to be lost; but, on this expedition, Tarleton burnt the house of Gen. Sumter, near Stateburgh,[3] and roused the spirit of the lion; at Camden, a party of his men cut to pieces Samuel Wiley, whom they mistook for his brother, John Wiley, then sheriff of the district, at his own house.[4] Governor Rutledge and his council again escaped Tarleton, by a few minutes, and by taking the road to Charlotte, in North Carolina. On the 1st of June, Sir Henry Clinton and Admiral Arbuthnot offered to the inhabitants, with some exceptions, "pardon for their past treasonable offences, and a reinstatement in their rights and immunities heretofore enjoyed, exempt from taxation, except by their own legislature." To many, this specious offer appeared to be all that they had been contending for; and they flocked in from all quarters to gain such high privileges. These, having signed declarations of allegiance, received protections as subjects, or were parolled to their plantations as prisoners of war. But, in the short space of twenty days, a second proclamation was issued, stating, that it was necessary for all persons to take an active part in securing his majesty's government, that all the inhabitants then prisoners on parole, except those taken at Charleston, and others in confinement, should be freed from their paroles, and restored to the rights of citizens; and all who neglected to return to their allegiance should be considered as rebels.

Nothing could have astonished the people more, than this last proclamation, those who had taken the paroles expected to remain on their plantations in security and ease; but now, they were called upon to return to their allegiance, and assist in securing his majesty's government. The purport of which was well understood; they were in fact to take up arms against their countrymen: at the very thought of which they were abhorrent. This crooked policy was no sooner adopted, than the British cause began to decline in South Carolina. The thread of the events above recorded, will now naturally lead us to the history of Marion's brigade. About the end of June, in this year, Capt. Ardesoif, of the British navy, arrived at Georgetown, to carry the last proclamation of Sir

Henry Clinton into effect, and invited the people to come in and swear allegiance to King George. Many of the inhabitants of that district submitted to this new act of degradation. But there remained a portion of it, stretching from the Santee to the Pedee, and including the whole of the present Williamsburgh, and part of Marion district, into which the British arms had not penetrated. The inhabitants of it were generally of Irish extraction; a people, who at all times during the war, abhorred either submission or vassalage. Among them, tradition has handed down the following story:—A public meeting was called, to deliberate upon their critical situation, and Major John James, who had heretofore commanded them in the field, and represented them in legislature, was selected as the person who should go down to Capt. Ardesoif, and know from him, whether, by his proclamation, he meant that they should take up arms against their countrymen. He proceeded to Georgetown, in the plain garb of a country planter, and was introduced to the captain, at his lodgings, a considerable distance from his ship. An altercation of the following nature took place. After the major had narrated the nature of his mission, the captain, surprised that such an embassy should be sent to him, answered, "the submission must be unconditional." To an inquiry, whether the inhabitants would not be allowed to stay at home, upon their plantations, in peace and quiet? he replied, "although you have rebelled against his majesty, he offers you a free pardon, of which you are undeserving, for you ought all to be hanged; but as he offers you a free pardon, you must take up arms in support of his cause." To Major James' suggesting that the people he came to represent would not submit on such terms, the captain, irritated at his republican language, particularly, it is supposed, at the word represent, replied, "you damned rebel, if you speak in such language I will immediately order you to be hanged up to the yard-arm."—The captain wore a sword, and Major James none, but perceiving what turn matters were likely to take, and not brooking such harsh language, he suddenly seized the chair on which he was seated, brandished it in the face of the captain, and making his retreat good through the back door of the house, mounted his horse, and made his escape into the country. This circumstance, apparently trivial, certainly hastened the rise of Marion's brigade. The story narrated, as now told, or embellished, always concluded in the same way: "you must take up arms in support of his majesty's cause." Many of the people of Williamsburgh had submitted and taken paroles, but to be obliged to imbrue their hands in the blood of their countrymen, was in their minds a breach of one of the commands of God, and they shuddered at the very thought.—They had besides, had two officers put over them, by the British commander, Amos Gaskens and John Hamilton; the first they despised on account of his petty larceny tricks, and the last they hated because of his profanity. About this time, news of the approach of Gates having arrived, a public meeting of this people was called, and it was unanimously resolved to take up arms in defence of

Chapter 2: Campaign of 1780

their country. Major James was desired to command them as heretofore, and they again arrayed themselves under their captains William M'Cottry, Henry Mouzon, John James,[5] of the lake, and John M'Cauley. The four companies, resolved on this great enterprise, consisted of about two hundred men. Shortly after, Col. Hugh Giles, of Pedee, proposed to join them, with two companies, Whitherspoon's and Thornly's; and his offer was gladly accepted. Gen. Gates had now arrived on the confines of the state, and in a consultation, held among these officers, it was agreed to send to him, to appoint them a commander. This was a wise resolution, and attended with the most salutary consequences. In the mean time, they made prisoners of Col. Cassels, Capt. Gaskens, and most of the officers appointed over them by the British, and took post at the pass of Lynch's creek, at Witherspoon's ferry. At this period, the tories on Lynch's creek, in the neighbourhood of M'Callum's ferry, had already begun their murders and depredations. Messrs. Matthew Bradley, Thomas Bradley, and John Roberts, respectable citizens, who had then joined neither party, and also, some others, were killed by them, in their own houses. These were headed by the two Harrisons, one afterwards a colonel, the other a major in the British service; whom Tarleton calls men of fortune. They were in fact two of the greatest banditti that ever infested the country. Before the fall of Charleston they lived in a wretched log hut, by the road, near M'Callum's, in which there was no bed-covering but the skins of wild beasts; during the contest the major was killed; but after it was over, the colonel retired to Jamaica, with much wealth, acquired by depredation. Capt. M'Cottry was now posted in advance of Witherspoon's ferry, at Indian town, and Col. Tarleton, having crossed at Lenud's ferry, and hearing of the Williamsburgh meeting, advanced, at the head of seventy mounted militia and cavalry, to surprise Major James. M'Cottry, first receiving notice of his movement, sent back for a reinforcement, and immediately marched his company, of about fifty mounted militia, to give him battle. Tarleton had been posted at dark, at the Kingstree, and M'Cottry approached him at midnight, but Tarleton marched away a few hours before he arrived. By means of the wife of Hamilton, the only tory in that part of the country, he had gained intelligence of M'Cottry's approach, as reported to him, with five hundred men.—The latter pursued, but, perhaps fortunately, without overtaking him. In this route Tarleton burnt the house of Capt. Mouzon; and after posting thirty miles, from Kingstree up to Salem, took Mr. James Bradley prisoner, the next day. Soon after this Lieut. Col. Hugh Horry arrived from Georgetown; and by right he would have had the command of Major James' party, but he declined it for some time. Of him more will be said hereafter. On the 10th or 12th of August, General Marion arrived at the post, at Lynch's creek, commissioned by Governor Rutledge to take the command of the party there, and a large extent of country on the east side of Santee. He was a stranger to the officers and men, and they flocked about him, to obtain a sight of their future commander.[6] He was rather below the middle stature of men, lean and swarthy. His body was well set, but his knees and ankles were badly formed; and he still limped upon one leg. He had a countenance remarkably steady; his nose was aquiline; his chin projecting; his forehead was large and high, and his eyes black and piercing. He was now forty-eight years of age; but still even at this age, his frame was capable of enduring fatigue and every privation, necessary for a partisan. His wisdom and patriotism will become henceforth conspicuous. Of a character, so much venerated, even trifles become important. He was dressed in a close round bodied crimson jacket, of a coarse texture, and wore a leather cap, part of the uniform of the second regiment, with a silver crescent in front, inscribed with the words, "Liberty or death." He was accompanied by his friend Col. Peter Horry, and some other officers. On the second or third day after his arrival, General Marion ordered his men to mount white cockades, to distinguish themselves from the tories, and crossed the Pedee, at Port's ferry, to disperse a large body of tories, under Major Ganey, stationed on Britton's neck, between great and little Pedee. He surprised them at dawn in the morning, killed one of their captains and several privates, and had two men wounded. Major James was detached at the head of a volunteer troop of horse, to attack their horse; he came up with them, charged, and drove them before him. In this affair, Major James singled out Major Ganey, (as he supposed) as the object of his single attack. At his approach Ganey fled, and he pursued him closely, and nearly within the reach of his sword, for half a mile; when behind a thicket, he came upon a party of tories, who had rallied. Not at all intimidated, but with great presence of mind, Major James called out, "Come on my boys!—Here they are!—Here they are!" And the whole body of tories broke again, and rushed into little Pedee swamp. Another party of tories lay higher up the river, under the command of Capt. Barefield; who had been a soldier in one of the South Carolina regiments. These stood to their ranks, so well, and appeared to be so resolute, that Gen. Marion did not wish to expose his men, by an attack on equal terms; he therefore feigned a retreat, and led them into an ambuscade, near the Blue Savannah, where they were defeated. This was the first manoeuvre of the kind, for which he afterwards became so conspicuous.

    Thus Gen. Marion, at once, fell upon employment, as the true way to encourage and to command militia; and their spirits began to revive. He returned to Port's ferry, and threw up a redoubt on the east bank of the Pedee, on which he mounted two old iron field pieces, to awe the tories. On the 17th of August, he detached Col. Peter Horry, with orders to take command of four companies, Bonneau's, Mitchell's, Benson's, and Lenud's, near Georgetown, and on the Santee; to destroy all the boats and canoes on the river, from the lower ferry to Lenud's; to post guards, so as to prevent all communication with Charleston, and to procure him twenty-five weight of gunpowder, ball

Chapter 2: Campaign of 1780

or buck shot, and flints in proportion. This order was made in pursuance of a plan he afterwards carried into effect; to leave no approach for the enemy into the district of which he had taken the command. The latter part of the order, shows how scanty were the means of his defence. There were few men, even in those days of enthusiasm, who would not have shrunk from such an undertaking. Gen. Marion himself marched to the upper part of Santee, it is believed, with the same object in view with which he had entrusted Horry. On his way he received intelligence of the defeat of Gates at Camden, and, without communicating it, he proceeded immediately towards Nelson's ferry. (16th August.) Near Nelson's, he was informed, by his scouts, that a guard, with a party of prisoners, were on their way to Charleston; and had stopped at the house, at the great Savannah, on the main road, east of the river. (20th of August.) It was night, and the general, a little before daylight next morning, gave the command of sixteen men to Col. Hugh Horry. He was ordered to gain possession of the road, at the pass of Horse creek, in the swamp, while the main body, under himself, was to attack in the rear. In taking his position, in the dark, Col. Horry advanced too near to a sentinel, who fired upon him. In a moment he rushed up to the house, found the British arms piled before the door, and seized upon them. Twenty-two British regulars, of the 63d regiment, two tories, one captain, and a subaltern were taken, and one hundred and fifty of the Maryland line, liberated. In his account of this affair Gen. Marion says he had one man killed, and Maj. Benson wounded. But the man, Josiah Cockfield, who was shot through the breast; lived to fight bravely again, and to be again wounded. In the account given of this action by Col. Tarleton, he says, contemptuously, the guard was taken by "a Mr. Horry"; but Gen. Marion, as commanding officer, is entitled to the credit of it. The news of the defeat of Gen. Gates now became public, and repressed all joy upon this occasion; no event which had yet happened, was considered so calamitous. An account of it will be given in his own words. Extract of a letter, from Gen. Gates, to the president of congress, dated Hillsborough, 20th August, 1780:—

"Sir, In the deepest distress and anxiety of mind, I am obliged to acquaint your excellency with the defeat of the troops under my command. I arrived with the Maryland line, the artillery, and the North Carolina militia, on the 13th inst. at Rugely's, thirteen miles from Camden; took post there, and was the next day joined by Gen. Stevens, with 700 militia from Virginia. The 15th, at daylight, I reinforced Colonel Sumter, with 300 North Carolina militia, 100 of the Maryland line, and two three-pounders from the artillery: having previously ordered him down from the Waxhaws, opposite to Camden, to intercept any stores coming to the enemy, and particularly troops coming from Ninety-Six. This was well executed by Col. Sumter. Having communicated my plan to the general officers in the afternoon of the 15th, it was resolved to march at ten at night, to take post in a very advantageous situation, with a deep creek in front, (Gum Swamp[7]) seven miles from Camden. At ten the army began to march, and having moved about five miles, the legion was charged by the enemy's cavalry, and well supported by Col. Porterfield, who beat back the enemy's horse, and was himself unfortunately wounded, (mortally) but the enemy's infantry advancing with a heavy fire, the troops in front gave way to the first Maryland brigade, and a confusion ensued which took some time to regulate. At length the army was ranged in line of battle. Gen. Gists' brigade on the right, close to a swamp; the North Carolina militia in the centre; the Virginia militia, the light infantry, and Porterfield's corps, on the left; the artillery divided to the brigades. The first Maryland brigade as a corps de reserve on the road. Col. Armand's corps was ordered to support the left flank. At daylight, they attacked and drove in our light party in front, when I ordered the left to advance and attack the enemy; but, to my astonishment, the left wing and North Carolina militia gave way. Gen. Caswell and myself, assisted by a number of officers, did all in our power to rally them; but the enemy's cavalry harassing their rear, they ran like a torrent, and bore all before them." This is all the general seemed to know of the action. Part of the brigade of North Carolina militia, commanded by Gen. Gregory, behaved well. They formed on the left of the continentals, and kept the field while their cartridges lasted. In bringing off his men, Gen. Gregory was thrice wounded by a bayonet, and several of his brigade, made prisoners, had no wounds but from the bayonet. The continental troops, under De Kalb and Gist, with inferior numbers, stood their ground and maintained the unequal conflict with great firmness. At one time they had taken a considerable body of prisoners; but at length, overpowered by numbers, they were compelled to leave the field. Tarleton's legion pursued the fugitives to the Hanging rock, fifteen miles, and glutted themselves with blood. Baron De Kalb, the second in command, an officer of great spirit, and long experience, was taken prisoner, after receiving eleven wounds, and died. Congress resolved that a monument should be erected to him at Annapolis. The gratitude of the people of Camden, has erected another in that town, and named a street De Kalb, after him.[8] Capts. Williams and Duval, of the Maryland troops, were killed; and Gen. Rutherford, of North Carolina, and Maj. Thomas Pinckney, of South Carolina, were wounded, and taken prisoners. Du Buysson, aid to Baron De Kalb, generously exposing himself to save his general, received several wounds and was taken. Lord Cornwallis states the force of Gates to have been six thousand men, and his own at near two thousand: a great disparity indeed. The loss of the Americans he calculates at between eight and nine hundred killed, and one thousand prisoners, many of whom were wounded; a number of colours, seven pieces of brass cannon, all the military stores and baggage, and one hundred and fifty waggons. His Lordship no doubt obtained a splendid victory; but tarnished it by his orders, issued soon after. Extract from the orders of Lord Cornwallis:—

Chapter 2: Campaign of 1780

"I have given orders, that the inhabitants of the province, who have taken part in this revolt, should be punished with the greatest rigour; and also those who will not turn out, that they may be imprisoned, and their property taken from them, or destroyed. I have likewise ordered, that compensation be made out of their estates, to the persons who have been injured or oppressed by them. I have ordered, in the most positive manner, that every militia man who has borne arms with us, and afterwards joined the army, shall be immediately hanged. I desire you will take the most rigourous measures to punish the rebels in the district in which you command; and that you obey in the strictest manner the directions I have given in this letter, relative to the inhabitants of this country." And wherever the British had garrisons or power these orders were carried into effect. Under them, at, or near Camden, Samuel Andrews, Richard Tucker, John Miles, Josiah Gayle, Eleazar Smith,——Sones, and many others, were hanged. Under them also, Cols. John Chesnut and Joseph Kershaw, Mr. James Brown, Mr. Strother, Mr. James Bradley, and a multitude of others, languished in irons, while their property was destroyed, and their families were starving. Yet Tarleton says of Lord Cornwallis, "He endeavoured so to conduct himself as to give offence to no party, and the consequence was that he was able entirely to please none." Of what kind of stuff must this man's heart have been made? But let us inquire a little further into the nature of these orders; which, in their extent, would have condemned to death, imprisonment and confiscation three fourths of the militia, who at that time, or afterwards, acted under the American standard in South Carolina. The proclamation of the British commanders of the 1st of June, 1780, before noticed, was either a snare to entrap the people into allegiance, and, as a necessary consequence, into recruits for their army; or it was terms of capitulation, fairly offered by the British commanders, to all such people as would submit to them. In other words, it was a solemn covenant.[9] If the proclamation was a snare, to bring the people to fight against their countrymen, as it has been generally thought, it was a breach of faith in those commanders, and not binding upon the people;[10] and the sooner they could avoid the treachery the better. Then, upon this view of the case, the more wicked were the orders of Lord Cornwallis, issued on the unsound principle of a faithless proclamation. Again, if it was intended as a covenant; as the paroles issued under it made them prisoners; the people, from the terms and the nature of it, ought to have been suffered to remain at home, in peace and quiet; for being prisoners, they could not, consistent with reason or principle, serve under those who held them in imprisonment. Further, the second proclamation declaring all paroles, after the 20th June, to be null and void, was an arbitrary change of what had been agreed upon by one party, the strongest, without the consent of the other; which, in the language of civilians, is odious.[11] Then the British commanders, having broken their covenant and declared it void, upon what principle could the people be punished by a breach of it? Upon none; for it did not exist. But further, the taking up arms in favour of the British, in nine cases out of ten, was compulsory; and could have no binding effect, either legally or morally speaking.

In addition to the enormity of the principle, upon which such men were to suffer, was the uncertainty of the law; for Lord Cornwallis' orders are so confusedly drawn, they will admit, as against the accused, of any latitude of construction: yet they denounce confiscation, imprisonment and death. Under the circumstances stated, the confiscations of Lord Cornwallis were robberies, his imprisonments were unjust and cruel, and his executions, always upon the gibbet, were military murders. And if, to gain his point, he did not, like the Duke of Alva, (employed in a similar vocation) make use of the rack, the stake, and the faggot, yet Lord Cornwallis resorted to every other mode of punishment, a more improved civilization had left him, to suppress civil liberty. Such was the character of the commander in chief of the British forces in South Carolina.

Now, we hold a generous foe entitled to favour and respect, and we shall hereafter bestow it, wherever due; but the interest of humanity requires, and it is a sacred trust, in the historian, that cruel domineering spirits should be fully exposed.

Soon after the affair at Nelson's, Gen. Marion marched back to Port's ferry. On the way, many of the militia, and all the liberated continentals, except three, deserted him. Two of these were Sergeants M'Donald and Davis, who were afterwards noted, the first for his daring spirit and address in single combat; the second, for his patient services, after being crippled by a wound. It is a real pleasure to record the virtues of men, who, serving in a subordinate capacity, never expected such virtues should be known. By the exertions of Gen. Marion and his officers, the spirits of the drooping militia began to revive. But about the 27th day of August, when, having the command of only one hundred and fifty men, he heard of the approach of Major Wemyss, above Kingstree, at the head of the 63d regiment, and a body of tories, under Maj. Harrison.

Maj. James was instantly despatched, at the head of a company of volunteers, with orders to reconnoitre, and count them. Col. Peter Horry was called in, and the general crossed Lynch's creek, and advanced to give battle. The night after Maj. James received his orders, the moon shone brightly, and by hiding himself in a thicket, close to their line of march, he formed a good estimate of the force of the enemy. As their rear guard passed, he burst from his hiding place, and took some prisoners. On the same night, about an hour before day, Marion met the major half a mile from his plantation. The officers immediately dismounted, and retired to consult, and the men sat on their horses in a state of anxious suspense. The conference was long and animated. At the end of it, an order was given to direct the march back to Lynch's creek, and no sooner was it given than a hollow groan might have been heard along the whole line. A bitter cup had now been mingled for the people of Williamsburgh

Chapter 2: Campaign of 1780

and Pedee; and they were doomed to drain it to the dregs: but in the end it proved a salutary medicine. Maj. James reported the British force to be double that of Marion's; and Ganey's party of tories in the rear, had always been estimated at five hundred men. In such a crisis, a retreat was deemed prudent. Gen. Marion recrossed the Pedee, at Port's; and the next evening, at the setting sun, commenced his retreat to North Carolina. (28th August, 1780.) He was accompanied by many officers, the names of all are not now recollected, and it may appear invidious to mention a few; the number of privates had dwindled down to sixty men. Capt. John James, with about ten chosen men, was left behind to succour the distressed, and to convey intelligence. The general's march, was, for some time, much impeded by the two field pieces, which he attempted to take along; but, after crossing the little Pedee, he wheeled them off to the right, and deposited them in a swamp; where they may since have amused the wondering deer hunter. This was the last instance of military parade evinced by the general. By marching day and night, he arrived at Amy's mill, on Drowning creek; whence he detached Maj. James, with a small party of volunteers, back to South Carolina, to gain intelligence, and to rouse the militia. Considering the distance back, and the British and tories in the rear, this was a perilous undertaking. The general continued his march, and pitched his camp for some time, on the east side of the White marsh, near the head of the Waccamaw.

At this place, the author had, (in the absence of his father,) the honour to be invited to dine with the general. The dinner was set before the company by the general's servant, Oscar, partly on a pine log, and partly on the ground; it was lean beef, without salt, and sweet potatoes. The author had left a small pot of boiled homminy in his camp, and requested leave of his host to send for it; and the proposal was acquiesced in, gladly. The homminy had salt in it, and proved, although eaten out of the pot, a most acceptable repast. The general said but little, and that was chiefly what a son would be most likely to be gratified by, in the praise of his father. They had nothing to drink but bad water; and all the company appeared to be rather grave.

At length Maj. James arrived. The news was, that the country through which Wemyss had marched, for seventy miles in length, and at places for fifteen miles in width, exhibited one continued scene of desolation. On most of the plantations every house was burnt to the ground, the negroes were carried off, the inhabitants plundered, the stock, especially sheep, wantonly killed; and all the provisions, which could be come at, destroyed. Fortunately the corn was not generally housed, and much of that was saved. Capt. James had fired upon a party at M'Gill's plantation; but it only increased the rage of the enemy. Adam Cusan had shot at the black servant of a tory officer, John Brockington, whom he knew, across Black creek. He was taken prisoner soon after, and for this offence, tried by a court martial, and, on the evidence of the negro, hanged. His wife and children prostrated themselves before Wemyss, on horseback, for a pardon; and he would have rode over them, had not one of his own officers prevented the foul deed; from this scene he proceeded on to superintend the execution. But these acts of wantonness and cruelty had roused the militia; and Maj. James reported they were ready to join the general. Marion, in a few days after, returned to South Carolina by a forced march. On the second day, while passing through the tory settlement, on Little Pedee, he traversed sixty miles, and arriving near Lynch's creek, was joined by Capts. John James and Henry Mouzon, with a considerable force. Here he was informed that a party of tories, but more numerous than his own, lay at Black Mingo, fifteen miles below, under the command of Capt. John Coming Ball. He might soon have been reinforced, but finding his men unanimous for battle, he gratified their wishes. The tories were posted at Shepherd's ferry, on the south side of Black Mingo, a deep navigable creek, and had command of the passage. To approach them, Gen. Marion was obliged to cross the creek, one mile above, over a boggy causeway and bridge of planks. It was nearly midnight when he arrived at the bridge; and while the party was crossing it, an alarm gun was heard in the tory camp. The general immediately ordered his men to follow him in full gallop, and, in a few minutes, they reached the main road which led to the ferry, about three hundred yards in front of it. Here they all dismounted, except a small body, which acted as cavalry. The general ordered a corps of supernumerary officers, under the command of Capt. Thomas Waties, to proceed down the road, and attack Dollard's house, where it was supposed the tories were posted, and at the same time he detached two companies to the right, under Col. Hugh Horry, and the cavalry to the left, to support the attack. Before the corps of officers could reach the house, the party on the right had encountered the enemy, who had left the house, and were drawn up in an old field opposite to it. This circumstance gave to the latter all the advantage of a surprise, and their first fire was so severe and unexpected, as to oblige Horry's men to fall back in some confusion; these were, however, soon rallied by the great exertions of Capt. John James. And the tories in the mean time being attacked on their flank by the corps of officers, and finding themselves between two fires, gave way after a few rounds, and took refuge in Black Mingo swamp, which was in their rear. This action, although of short duration, was so closely and sharply contested, that the loss on both sides was nearly one third, killed and wounded.

 Capt. George Logan, of Charleston, had been sick near the White marsh; but, hearing that Marion had marched for South Carolina, he rose from his bed, mounted his horse, and rode eighty miles the day before the action, to join him, and was killed that night at Black Mingo. Such was the energy of this fallen patriot. Two other gallant officers, Capt. Henry Mouzon and his Lieut. Joseph Scott, were, by their wounds, rendered unfit for further service.

Chapter 2: Campaign of 1780

Many of the enemy had been lately companions in arms with Marion, and in a short time joined him again, and behaved well afterwards. As many of his party had left their families in much distress, the general gave them leave to go to their homes, and appointed them to meet him at Snow's island, on the Pedee. They delayed so long, that he began to despair of their coming, and proposed to a few officers, who were with him, to abandon South Carolina, and join Gen. Greene, at Charlotte. But Col. Hugh Horry, who was his bosom friend, and partook more of his confidence than any other man, prevailed upon him to remain. The services of Col. Hugh Horry, in the field, were certainly highly meritorious; but he never rendered his country more effectual aid than by this act of friendly persuasion. The militia at length came in. The general soon after, marched up into Williamsburgh, and gained reinforcements daily. His first intention was to chastise Harrison, on Lynch's creek; and he was moving up for that purpose, but hearing that Col. Tynes had summoned the people of Salem, and the fork of Black river, out to do duty as his majesty's subjects, he instantly resolved to break up the party, before its newly made converts should become confirmed in the principles they had unwillingly adopted.—Tynes lay encamped at Tarcote, in the fork of Black river, much off his guard, and Gen. Marion crossing the lower ford of the northern branch of that river, at Nelson's plantation, marched up and surprised him in the night. The rout was universal, and attended, as Tarcote swamp was near, with more dismay than slaughter. Gen. Marion lost not a man; some tories were killed, and among the rest Capt. Amos Gaskens; a man noted before the war for petty larceny, and after it commenced, for plundering under Major Wemyss. The most of Tynes' men, soon after joined Gen. Marion, and fought bravely.

The next enemy Gen. Marion proceeded to encounter was the renowned Col. Tarleton. Hearing that he had left Charleston, where he had been for some time past confined with a fever, and that he was to cross at Nelson's ferry with a body of cavalry, Gen. Marion lay in wait for him, in the river swamp, a part of two days. (Nov. 1780.) He had cut bushes, and planted them on the road side in such a manner as would have ensured him a deadly fire. But in the evening of the second day, he was informed that Tarleton had passed before he had arrived on his way to Camden; and the general immediately commenced his march up the road in the same direction. In the night he stopped in a wood, near where Mr. Charles Richardson now lives, and was about to encamp; but seeing a great light towards Gen. Richardson's plantation, he concluded that it was the houses of the plantation on fire, and that Tarleton was there. While deliberating what was to be done, Col. Richard Richardson came in, and informed him the enemy was there, and at least double his number, with two field pieces; and it was discovered that one of his men had deserted to them. Finding Tarleton had now a guide, and that his position was unsafe, Marion immediately retreated; and crossing the Woodyard, then a tremendous swamp, in the most profound darkness,[12] he never stopped till he had passed Richbourgh's mill dam, on Jack's creek, distant about six miles. Having now a mill pond and miry swamp between him and the enemy, and the command of a narrow pass, the first words the general was heard to say were, "Now we are safe!" As soon as Tarleton received intelligence of Gen. Marion's position, and had got a guide, he thought to make sure of his prey, and commenced his march: he was led in silence to the spot which he contemplated as another scene of slaughter; but his intended victim had flown. He pursued to the Woodyard, but could not pass that night. The next morning Marion, knowing the vigilance of his foe, decamped betimes; and pursuing his route down Black river, for thirty-five miles, through woods, and swamps and bogs, where there was no road, encamped the following night on advantageous ground, at Benbow's ferry, now Lowry's bridge, about ten miles above Kingstree, on the east side of Black river. In a partisan warfare this position was the best that could have been taken. He could now defend himself, first at Black river itself; and after that at three difficult passes, of swamps, in his rear; all within ten miles, on that side of the river, before he reached Kingstree; but on the direct road to that place, on the west, there was but the one defile at the river; besides the possibility of being overtaken before he reached it. Here then Marion determined to make a stand, and felled trees across the road to impede the enemy. On the morning after the retreat, Tarleton found Marion's trail across the Woodyard, but went round it, and pursued, as he says, "for seven hours, through swamps and defiles." In fact he pursued about twenty-five miles, when arriving at Ox swamp,[13] which was wide and miry, and without a road to pass it, he desisted, saying to his men, "Come my boys! let us go back, and we will soon find the game cock, (meaning Sumter) but as for this d——d old fox, the devil himself could not catch him." After this, the two generals were thus characterized. It is amusing to read Tarleton's pompous account of this pursuit. He insinuates that Marion's sole view was to save himself; as Tarleton stopped ten or twelve miles short of Benbow's, he might not have heard of the preparations made there to receive him. For the same distance Marion had been skirting the south branch of Black river, and could at any time, in a few minutes, have plunged into it, and no regular body of cavalry could have followed him. Had Tarleton proceeded with his jaded horses to Benbow's, he would have exposed his force to such sharp shooting as he had not yet experienced, and that in a place where he could not have acted either with his artillery or cavalry.

    On this expedition, Tarleton burnt the house, out houses, corn and fodder, and a great part of the cattle, hogs and poultry, of the estate of Gen. Richardson. The general had been active with the Americans, but was now dead; and the British leader, in civilized times, made his widow and children suffer for the deeds of the husband and parent, after the manner of the East, and coast of Barbary. What added to the cruel nature of the act, was that he had first dined

Chapter 2: Campaign of 1780

in the house, and helped himself to the abundant good cheer it afforded. But we have seen before the manner in which he requited hospitality. It was generally observed of Tarleton and his corps, that they not only exercised more acts of cruelty than any one in the British army, but also carried further the spirit of depredation.

The wise policy of Gen. Marion had hitherto been to keep his own party, as yet but small, constantly in motion, and thus to multiply it, in the view of the enemy; and immediately to strike at all other parties preparing to join them. Had parties from the country been suffered to incorporate with the British, and to unite in their principles and views, the sense of a dereliction of duty, and the punishment expected to await it, as well as the pride of opinion, usually attending a new conversion, might have kept them firm in their apostacy. Of a truth, Gen. Marion made many converts to the cause of his country.

Many from inclination and principle felt a strong desire to join him, and again to reconcile themselves to the cause they had at first adopted and deserted with the utmost reluctance, and became confirmed in their views, by his apparent abilities and successes; others had felt the suddenness and unexpected severity of his midnight blows, and thought the step of uniting with him would be the most prudent or politic. From the operation of both sentiments, the people of that tract of country, on a line, stretching from Camden across to the mouth of Black creek, on Pedee, including generally both banks of the Wateree, Santee and Pedee, down to the sea coast, were now (excepting Harrison's party on Lynch's creek) either ready or preparing to join Gen. Marion. Many had already served under him, within the lines of the British or tories, and submitted to all the subsequent losses; which although the more to their credit, it is now much to be regretted, that they cannot be particularized. As to the people of old Cheraw district, above the line designated, and especially on the Pedee, they were at this time under their leader Gen. Thomas, waging an exterminating warfare with the tories on their borders; which still remains, and it is more than probable ever will remain, unrecorded.

From Benbow's ferry, Gen. Marion's first expedition was planned against Georgetown. The formidable enemy he had nearly encountered, had not diminished his energies. Georgetown, at that period, and afterwards, was often the point to which his views were directed; since it was there only he expected to take the supplies of ammunition, clothing and salt, which he sorely wanted. To expedite his scheme he crossed Black river, at Potato ferry, a retired place, and proceeded on towards Georgetown by the Gap way.—Three miles from the town there is a swamp called White's bay,[14] which discharges itself by two mouths, the one into Black river, the other into Sampit, thus insulating the town. Over the one, which empties itself into Sampit, there is a bridge, two miles from Georgetown, called White's bridge. Back of these swamps, Gen. Marion took his stand, near a place called the Camp, above the bridge. Here he despatched Col. P. Horry towards the Black river, and Capt. John Melton to the Sampit road, both leading into the town, to reconnoitre. At White's plantation, Horry fell in with Capt. Merritt, who, with a few dragoons, was escorting a couple of ladies from Georgetown; Merritt, after defending himself bravely, escaped and gave the alarm. Melton, unfortunately, came in contact with a party of tories, under Barefield, much larger than his own, who were patroling near the bridge. A few shots were exchanged, and Melton was compelled to retreat. But in this short affair Gabriel Marion, nephew of the general, had his horse killed under him, and was taken prisoner; but as soon as his name was announced, he was inhumanely shot. The instrument of death was planted so near that it burnt his linen at the breast. He had been a lieutenant in the second regiment, was a young gentleman of good education, of whom high expectations were formed, and who was much beloved in the brigade. As the general had no children, he mourned over this nephew, as would a father over an only son; but he soon recollected that he had an example to set, and shortly after publicly expressed this consolation for himself—that his nephew was a virtuous young man—that he had fallen in the cause of his country, and he would mourn over him no more. At the same time Mr. Swaineau, a worthy man, was killed. Ere this, he had exercised the peaceful profession of a schoolmaster; but finding there was no employment for him in these perilous times, he had boldly shouldered the musket, and died a soldier. But so prone are mankind to pass over the merits of this most useful class of men, that had he not fallen by the side of a Marion, perhaps his memory would have been forgotten. About the same time, Mr. Bentley, another schoolmaster, was killed in action. The suspension of all public education, which led to the fate of such men, and the discontinuance of all religious worship, hereafter more particularly noticed, are striking instances of the calamitous state of the country during this period.

The British in Georgetown being now alarmed, Gen. Marion's wise scheme to surprise them was frustrated; and he retired to Snow's island. This island became henceforth the most constant place of his encampment; a secure retreat, a depot for his arms and ammunition; and, under similar pressures, a second Athelney, from which he might sally out upon the modern, but no less ferocious plunderers than their ancestors, the Danes. Snow's island, not quite so marshy as was the retreat of the great Alfred, lies at the confluence of Lynch's creek and the Pedee. On the east flows the Pedee; on the west Clark's creek, a navigable stream, issuing from Lynch's creek above; and on the north lies Lynch's creek, nearly choked up by rafts of logs, but wide and deep. The island is high river swamp, and large, of itself affording much provision and live stock, as did all the Pedee river swamp at that day. In places, there were open cultivated lands on the island; but it was much covered by thick woods and cane brakes; it was also near to Ganey's party of tories; and by crossing the river, and marching two or three hours, Marion could forage in an enemy's

Chapter 2: Campaign of 1780

country. All these advantages were well suited to the views of such a leader as Gen. Marion; and the reader is to bear in mind that such was the kind of swamps he commonly occupied. Reinforcements were now coming in to him daily, and his party began at this time to assume the appearance and force of a brigade. He lay here to receive them, and to repose his men, and horses; which, from the time he left the White marsh until he halted at Snow's island, had passed over at least three hundred and sixty miles, in rapid marches and counter marches, made principally in the night. Marion now kept out a strict watch upon the enemy. About this time, Lieut. Roger Gordon was sent out with a party, to patrole on Lynch's creek, and stopped at a house for provisions and refreshments. While there, he was attacked by Capt. Butler with a much larger party of tories, who having succeeded in making good his approaches to the house, set it on fire. Gordon then capitulated on a promise of quarters; but no sooner had his party grounded their arms, than they were all put to death. Not long after, Col. Kalb, Mr. Thomas Evans and some others, were murdered by Gibson, a coloured man, and his party of tories, in a manner still more shocking to humanity. In the dead of night, Kalb's own house was surrounded, and set on fire; he, his wife, and family, and some neighbours were in it, and in bed, when awaking, they sued for quarters. Gibson promised that they should not be hurt, if they surrendered; but as soon as the men had passed out into the light of the conflagration, they were all shot. We have some time since mentioned the murder of the two Bradleys, and others, on Lynch's Creek, and lately that of Gabriel Marion. Such provocations were no longer to be borne. Henceforth, there commenced such a bloody warfare between the whigs and tories, as is seldom recorded in the annals of even civil commotion.[15] Besides the provocations mentioned, when a tory was taken prisoner, there were no means of securing him, and he commonly soon made his escape, and thereafter became a guide to his associates. It was not so with whigs who were made prisoners, for they could be sent to Georgetown or Camden. But now, seldom were prisoners made on either side, and if made, that was no security for their lives: they were sure to be put to death, either openly or privately, by a few infuriated men, who could be subjected to no subordination. Enough is said. Let the rest be buried in oblivion.

At and near Snow's island, Gen. Marion secured what boats he wanted; and burnt those more remote. To prevent the approach of an enemy, he fell upon a plan of insulating as much as possible the country under his command. For this purpose he broke down bridges, and felled trees across causeways and difficult passes. As there was no market in that day, and the vicinity of a road was dangerous, the inhabitants aided him much in this design. History furnishes innumerable instances of the good effect of such a system of defensive warfare. His scouting parties moved principally in the night, and in all directions, and to whatever course they turned an enemy was easily found.

The British had posts at Nelson's ferry, Scott's lake, and Georgetown; and the tories on Lynch's creek, and Little Pedee, were more numerous, but not so well directed as Marion's party.

Col. P. Horry and Maj. John Postell, with detachments, were posted, the first on Waccamaw creek, the second on the neck between Black and Pedee rivers, with orders to take all boats and canoes, and all horses, from friends or foes; to impress negroes as boat hands and pioneers, to seize all arms and ammunition, to prevent provisions from being sent to the enemy in Georgetown, and to send up as much rice and salt to Snow's island, as possible. (30th Dec. 1780.) All who would not join them were to be taken prisoners, and all who supplied the enemy with stock, or grain, were to be treated as traitors. Thus martial law was fully established, and, for self defence, never was it more necessary. When Gen. Marion himself, or any of his parties, left the island on an expedition, they almost invariably struck into the woods towards the heads of the larger water courses, and crossed them near their source; and if in haste, they swam over them. Many of the general's trails remained for a long time after, and some are now roads. When it is said hereafter that Gen. Marion crossed a river, for instance the Santee, it is not to be understood that he stopped, like Caesar at the Rhine, to build a bridge over it; or that he was provided with the convenient modern apparatus of pontoons, or oftentimes with a common flat; even the last would have been too slow for the usual rapidity of his motions. He seldom waited for more than a single canoe, along side of which his sorrel horse Ball,[16] was usually led into the river, and he floated over like an amphibious animal. The rest of the horses soon learned to follow instinctively. Where a canoe was not to be had, the general swam over frequently on the back of this uncommon horse. No leader, in ancient or modern times, ever passed rivers with more rapidity. His plans were laid, and his movements conducted, with the most uncommon secrecy. After making a movement, his most confidential officers and men have had to search for him for days together, perhaps without finding him. His scouts, when returning, and at a loss, used a loud and shrill whistle, as a signal; which could be heard in the night to an astonishing distance. It is well described in Scott's Lady of the Lake:

> "He whistled shrill,
> And he was answered from the hill;
> Wild as the scream of the curlew,
> From crag to crag, the signal flew."

As an instance of the secrecy with which Gen. Marion's plans were always adopted and conducted, the following may be regarded as a specimen in his progress throughout. His men having been several times unexpectedly led out

Chapter 2: Campaign of 1780

upon long expeditions, without preparation, and suffering for the want of food on such occasions, after some time, were in the habit of watching his cook, and if they saw him unusually busied in preparing any of the frugal fare then in use, they prepared accordingly. The general's favourite time for moving was at the sitting sun, and then it was expected the march would continue all night. But the present time, and afterwards, before striking any sudden blow, he has been known to march sixty or seventy miles, without taking any other refreshment, than a meal of cold potatoes and a drink of cold water, in twenty-four hours. During this period men were but badly clothed in homespun, which afforded little warmth. They slept in the open air, according to their means, either with or without a blanket. They had nothing but water to drink. They fed chiefly upon sweet potatoes, either with or without fresh beef. And they submitted to this without a murmur; but all sighed for salt! for salt! that first article of necessity for the human race. Little do the luxurious of the present day know of the pressure of such a want. Salt was now ten silver dollars the bushel, when brought more than thirty miles from the Waccamaw sea shore, where it was coarsely manufactured. It was harder to get one silver dollar then, than ten now; so that on a low calculation, a bushel of coarse bay salt, sold at that time for one hundred dollars value of the present day. As soon as Gen. Marion could collect a sufficient quantity of this desirable article at Snow's island, he distributed it out in quantities, not exceeding a bushel to each whig family; and thus endeared himself the more to his followers.

Thus closed the year one thousand seven hundred and eighty, over the head of Gen. Marion. We will leave him for a moment, to such repose as the island afforded, and state some matters to carry on the chain of events.

On the 12th July, General Sumter commenced his brilliant career. On the west of the Catawba, he defeated a large party of tories, and a party of British, and killed Col. Ferguson, who commanded the former, and Capt. Huck, at the head of the latter. This man had shocked the good Presbyterians in that part of the country by his profanity; he burnt their church, their parsonage, and their bibles, and treated them with insult and cruelty. About the 30th July, Gen. Sumter nearly annihilated the Prince of Wales' regiment, and routed a large body of tories at the Hanging rock.—Soon after the defeat of Gates, the enemy was left at liberty to turn a greater force upon Sumter, and his men, being worn down by fatigue and want of sleep, he was surprised and defeated at Fishing creek, by Tarleton, but with little loss, for he rallied his forces in three days after.[17] On the 12th Nov. Major Wemyss attempted to surprise him near the Fishdam ford, on Broad river, at the head of a corps of infantry and dragoons. Col. Thomas Taylor, with his regiment, was posted in advance, and his men lay securely at their fires, thinking the enemy at a distance. But the colonel, from what has been termed a presentiment, was uneasy and could not rest; he got up, and hearing the barking of dogs and some other unusual noises, he woke up his men, and removed them back from their fires. Soon after, the British appeared at them, and thus offered themselves to the aim of experienced marksmen. In the mean time Sumter came up to their aid, and the enemy was totally defeated. Major Wemyss was severely wounded and taken. He had in his pocket a list of the houses he had burnt at Williamsburgh and Pedee; with great trepidation he showed it to Sumter, and begged he would protect him from the militia.—Notwithstanding his atrocities he was treated with indulgence; but became a cripple for life. On the 20th of the same month Sumter was attacked by Col. Tarleton, at Black Stocks. The action was severe, and of the British officers, Major Money, and Lieuts. Gibson and Cape, were killed. Sumter lost few men, but he was himself wounded. The ball passed through the shoulder and carried away a small portion of the backbone. He was placed in a raw bullock's hide, fastened between two horses, and thus carried with a guard of five men to the mountains.

Tarleton, as usual, sent an account of his victory, much exaggerated, to Lord Cornwallis, who writes to him on the 22d of the same month: "I most heartily wish you joy of your success, but wish it had not cost you so much." And again, on the next day: "I shall be very glad to hear that Sumter is in a condition to give us no further trouble; he certainly has been our greatest plague in this country." The inhabitants of the New Acquisition, now York district, were among the warm friends of Gen. Sumter; it was among these people he generally recruited his forces. They never submitted to the British nor took protection. The most distinguished leaders, under Sumter, were Colonels Niel, Hill, Lacey, Winn, Bratton, Brandon, and Majors Davie and Winn. Davie commanded a corps of cavalry, which was never surprised nor dispersed during the war.

In the summer of 1780, Col. Ferguson, of the British 71st, had undertaken to visit the tory settlements in the upper country, and train up the young men to arms. Among these several unprincipled people had joined him, and acted with their usual propensity for rapine and murder. Many Americans, fleeing before them, passed over into the state of Tennessee, then beginning to be settled. By their warm representations, they roused the spirit of the people of that country, which has since become so often conspicuous. Although safe from any enemy but the savages of their cane brakes, they left their families, and generously marched to the assistance of their friends. Nine hundred of them mounted, under the command of Col. Campbell, poured down from the Allegany, like the torrents from its summit. Gunpowder they had already learnt to prepare from the saltpetre in their caves, and lead they dug out of their mines. Dried venison satisfied their hunger, pure water slaked their thirst, and at the side of a rock they enjoyed comfortable repose. Armed with rifles, sure to the white speck on the target, at the distance of one hundred paces, or to decapitate the wild turkey on the top of the tallest pine—these were indeed a formidable band.

Chapter 2: Campaign of 1780

Their other leaders were Shelby, Sevier, Williams and Cleveland, all inured to the pursuit of the savage or the wild beast of the forest. Thus equipped and commanded, and with such few wants, they moved rapidly on to attack Ferguson, a no less formidable foe, and on the 7th of October, 1780, reached him, strongly posted on King's mountain. Campbell divided his men into three bands, one under himself, one under Cleveland, and the other under Shelby.—Cleveland commenced the attack, and fired until Ferguson, advancing sufficiently near, ordered the British to charge with bayonets; before these he retired. By this time Shelby had ascended the mountain, and gave an unexpected and deadly fire. The bayonet had scarcely been again successful, when Campbell reached the summit and fired in another and more destructive volley. Ferguson presented a new front, and the bayonet again prevailed. But Cleveland had rallied his men and poured in the fourth fire: and now as often as one American party was driven back, another returned to the attack, and as victory was becoming sure, with more determined resolution. The unconquerable spirit of Ferguson still refused to submit, but baited thus, as he was on all sides, resistance became vain. At length this distinguished officer received a mortal wound, and falling upon the field, his second in command, Capt. Abraham De Peyster, sued for quarters. Eleven hundred of the enemy were killed, wounded or taken, of which one hundred were British. The Americans lost but few men, but among these were Col. Williams and Major Chronicle. Thus, through the successes of Sumter and Marion, and this brilliant achievement, towards the close of this memorable year the drooping spirits of the people began to revive, and men flocked on all sides to the standard of their country.

* * * * *

Detached Narratives for 1780

As these are intended to be unconnected, and entirely miscellaneous, they will be inserted without much regard to time or place. We have just recorded the fate of the distinguished Ferguson, and the first meed of praise is due to him. Yes! reader, praise to a generous enemy! He was a major, and commanded a rifle corps during the campaign of Washington, in New Jersey. On one occasion Gen. Washington rode out with a few French and American officers to reconnoitre, and Ferguson, with his riflemen, lay in a wood near to the road by which they both went and returned. Washington was conspicuous from his stature, and uniform, and the grey horse which he rode. He passed hard by the corps, at an easy canter, and Ferguson's men were preparing to fire upon him, when their leader prevented the act. Who would not hereafter applaud the character of Ferguson? In a letter which he wrote to a friend, that contains this narrative, he mentions he was glad he did not know it was Gen.

Washington at the time, lest he should have been tempted to fire at him. But the same generous spirit which prevented it in the one case, would, it is more than probable, have actuated him in the other.

The next meed of praise is certainly due to friendship. In this action the hon. Robert Stark, then a boy of fourteen, was among the American combatants. Like a war worn veteran he was seen firing his rifle and encouraging others to the onset. It was here that, actuated by the cause of his country, and the rigourous confinement of his father in irons, he first avenged himself of the enemy. His next battle was at the Cowpens, where he acted as an adjutant under Gen. Pickens.

During the time General Marion lay at the White marsh, Capt. Gavin Witherspoon, of Pedee, with three or four men, were concealing themselves in Pedee swamp: in the night he discovered a camp of the tories, whom he had reason to think were in pursuit of him, and watched them till they had all fallen asleep; he proposed to his men to attack them, but they were fearful of numbers. He then declared he would take them himself. Creeping up cautiously, he found that they had encamped at the butt of a pine, blown up by the roots, and that their guns were piled up against a limb, at the distance of forty or fifty feet from them. He continued to creep till he got possession of their guns, and then called to them loudly to surrender. Not knowing his force, they did so, and Witherspoon's men came to his assistance and tied them, in number seven. Gavin, and John Witherspoon, his brother, were two active spirited men at this period. They succeeded each other as captains in the neck between Pedee and Lynch's creek; and at the call of danger were generally foremost. After Capt. Baxter was promoted to be major, Thomas Potts was elected captain of the upper Pedee company; he had been captain in the rifle regiment of state troops, and was a brave soldier and firm patriot.

Major Wemyss, in laying waste the country, was particularly inimical to looms and sheep; no doubt that he might deprive the inhabitants of the means of clothing themselves. What sheep he did not kill for the use of his men, he ordered to be bayoneted. He burnt the Presbyterian church at Indiantown; because, as he said, it was a sedition shop. Before a house was burnt, permission was seldom given to remove the furniture. When he came to Maj. James' he was met by his lady with much composure. He wished to bring her husband to submission, and said to her, "If he would come in and lay down his arms, he should have a free pardon." She replied, "As to that she could not have any influence over him. That times were such he was compelled to take a part, and he had taken that of his country." Wemyss after this had her and her children locked up in a chamber, from whence they did not come out, for two days and a half; and until the house was about to be burnt. Capt. David Campbell (of Edisto,) carried with his own hands, food and other refreshments to a back window for her, apparently unknown to Wemyss. Capt. John James, son of

Chapter 2: Campaign of 1780

the major, had been taken in Charleston, and paroled. He was ordered into custody, with the threat, that "If he was found to have broken his parole, he would be hanged in the morning to yonder tree." Accordingly a court martial sat over him in the morning. The witnesses called were his own and his father's negroes; but, strange to tell, no evidence was given against him, and he was acquitted. Such were the mock trials of the British. As, when we come to speak of the battle of Eutaw, there will be many chiefs of higher title to be named, it is but justice to Capt. James now to mention, that before that time he was exchanged, and fought there with much bravery, as an adjutant. As there was no trade or intercourse between that part of the country and a market, people were to be seen, after the fires, searching for every thing they could find, knife blades, scissors, hinges, nails, &c. Handles were put to the knives, dishes and plates were rudely manufactured out of wood, and log huts were gradually built by the assistance of one another. Many negroes were taken out of Williamsburgh; these were afterwards recovered by Maj. James. Directly after the retreat of Rawdon from Camden, he, at the head of five or six men, passed through the country from Santee to an island near Beaufort, where he found and brought away one hundred and fifty, all plundered from his own neighbourhood. This account has been inserted here, that the chain of events might not hereafter be broken.

It is stated, (page 45,)[18] that Col. Tarleton took Mr. James Bradley prisoner; the manner in which this was done, and the subsequent treatment of Bradley, are well deserving a place in this narrative. After being chased from his breakfast, thirteen miles below, by M'Cottry, Tarleton and a few officers came to Bradley's at midday, passed himself as Col. Washington, and requested an early dinner. Bradley provided dinner for him, and unsuspectingly communicated to him the plans of his countrymen. After dinner, Tarleton asked him to guide him over two difficult fords across two branches of Black river, near his house; Bradley consented, and after they had passed Magirt's swamp, Tarleton told him he was a prisoner. A wild Arab would not have treated him thus. Bradley, though circumvented in this manner, was a wise but unsuspicious man; and before that had much influence in the legislature. He was sent to Camden gaol, and confined in heavy irons; he was often carted to the gallows and saw others executed; he expected death, and was prepared for it; but he had many friends in Marion's brigade, and it was well known to the enemy that his execution would have been severely retaliated. He was not released from gaol until the 10th of May the next year, when Rawdon retreated from Camden; and he bore the marks of the irons until his death. Being requested, on one occasion he showed these to the author, then a youth, and said, "If the good of your country requires the sacrifice, be ready to suffer imprisonment and death in its cause." Soon after his confinement, Mrs. Bradley petitioned Tarleton to liberate her husband, but he treated her with scurrilous language and great brutality. This man, who had been treated by Mrs. Bradley to a plentiful meal, after he had fasted for twenty-four hours, and when he and his followers were fainting with fatigue and want, had now the impudence and cruelty to call her by the grossest names in the vocabulary of bilingsgate. Mrs. Bradley! one of the most humane, gentle and affectionate of her sex, who would willingly have offered him bread in his true character. Tarleton even denied her admittance with her supplies to her husband; and she sought and obtained it elsewhere.

To people of good feelings, but particularly the religious, this period (1780 and 1781) was truly distressing. From the time of the fall of Charleston, all public education was at an end, and soon after, all public worship was discontinued. Men from sixty years of age, down to boys of fourteen, (few of whom dared to stay at home) were engaged in active and bloody warfare. These had their minds in constant occupation, which, in whatever moral situation a man may be placed, brings with it a certain degree of satisfaction, if not contentment. All were actuated by the love of country, and but few by the love of fame: and next to the duties of religion, the exercise of those of patriotism excites the highest energy and brings the most sublime satisfaction to the human mind. But to the female sex, and the superannuated of the male, little consolation of that nature could be afforded. Even these were exposed to that kind of danger which might be inflicted by brutality at home, and most of them had relatives in the field to whom they were bound by the most tender and sacred ties, who were subjected to constant dangers, and for whose fate they were unceasingly anxious.—There was no place for the pleasures of society, for in the country these were too remote from a home that must constantly be watched. As a comfort in this situation females employed themselves in domestic occupations, in which that of the distaff had a considerable share, and all might indeed have exercised their private devotions; but that faint picture of heaven, that sweet consolation which is derived from associating with one's friends in public worship, was wholly denied them. Most of the churches in towns and the country, were either burnt or made depots for the stores of the enemy; some in fact were converted into stables; and of the remainder, all in the country were closed.—In a warfare of such atrocity there was little safety in any situation where numbers were collected, and as we have seen that the tories, by their murders, violated the sanctity of private dwellings, how then could it be expected they would be awed by the holiness of a church? In a camp, where was no permanency and but little rest, there was no place for chaplains,[19] and at home there was not security even for pious pastors; consequently, as the most prudent course, they generally went into exile. Among these one shall be mentioned, the Rev. Dr. Thomas Reese, of Salem, on Black river. It was in his congregation that the murders perpetrated by Harrison and his followers first began, and three respectable men of his flock had already fallen victims to civil rage. Had he gone about to administer comfort out of his own family, it would have been termed sedition, and Dr. Reese would have made himself a voluntary martyr. He took the wiser course of retiring with his family before the storm, and under many privations, continued to preach. In theology, modern philosophy, and all the sciences connected with his profession he was deeply read. For classic literature, which it is so common for the superficial to decry, he was a great advocate, and to evince his sincerity retained his knowledge of the dead languages as long as he lived. In his discourses he was neither an extempore preacher, nor did he read. He wrote out his sermons correctly, and then committing them carefully to memory, left the copy at home, and afterwards delivered them from the pulpit with all the energy of extemporary preaching, and so tenacious was his memory that he was never known to faulter. He wrote many excellent sermons, all of which except two, preserved in the American Preacher, and those not his best, are believed to be lost. He also wrote an essay "on the influence of religion in civil society", which, from Princeton college, where he was educated, obtained for him the degree of Doctor of Divinity. But like most American productions, it was soon neglected, and did not pass into a second edition. In contemplating the meek and unobtrusive virtues of this pious man, we do not hesitate to say he was a pattern of Christian charity, as nearly resembling his divine master as has been seen in modern times. The author knew him well for several years after the peace of 1782; he was his friend and tutor, and he owes to Dr. Reese the highest obligations, and to his memory the most profound respect.

Footnotes

1. Two boys, Francis G. Deliesseline and Samuel Dupre, had the boldness to undertake, and did recover fourteen of White's cavalry horses from the British, and delivered them to Major Jamieson in Georgetown, refusing a reward he offered.

2. See Dr. Brownfield's account of this affair, which throws more light upon it, than any thing heretofore written. Appendix, p. 1. To paliate his conduct, Tarleton has written a most partial account of it, which has been followed by Moultrie, and substantially by Ramsay. The faults committed by Buford, he says, were his sending his baggage ahead, and not firing till the cavalry were within ten steps.—But Buford, notwithstanding all the odium excited against him by his ill fortune, was tried by a court martial, and acquitted. Tarleton excuses his cruelty, by stating, that his horse was knocked down, at the first fire: and his men, thinking him killed, to avenge his death, were more sanguinary than usual, and he was unable, from that circumstance, for a while to restrain them. But Lord Cornwallis approved the whole, and praised and caressed Tarleton, while he was fortunate.

3. The proper name is Stateburgh. But so great is the propensity of Americans for introducing the S into the already hissing English language, that it is now written commonly Statesburgh.

4. Tarleton despatched his favourite sergeant Hutt, who always charged by his side, with a sergeant's guard, to perform this deed. The visit was quite unexpected by Wiley. In going up to his house, two men were left concealed, behind two large gate posts, at the entrance of the yard; while Hutt, with the rest, broke into the house abruptly; he demanded Wiley's shoe buckles, and while he stooped down to unbuckle them, the wretch Hutt aimed a stroke with his sword at his head. Wiley, seeing the gleam of the descending weapon, parried the blow from his head, by his hand, with the loss of some fingers; then, springing out of the door, he ran for the gate, where the two concealed men despatched him with many blows. The cause of offence was, that John Wiley, as sheriff, had superintended the execution of some men under the existing state laws, at that time against treason. After the battle of Cowpens Hutt disappeared.

5. He was second cousin to the major. Of this family, there were five brothers, than whom no men under Marion were more brave; these were John, William, Gavin, Robert and James. Gavin died a few weeks since, with whom the family became extinct. More of Gavin and Robert hereafter. 20th July, 1821.

6. He was not appointed a general till some time after this, but as we have not the date of his commission, henceforth he will be styled general; and his other officers, to avoid repetitions, are designated generally by the rank they held at the disbandment of the brigade.

7. Had Gen. Gates reached the important pass of Gum Swamp, and occupied it properly, the fortune of war might have been changed. It is a miry creek, impassible for many miles, except at the road. He missed it only by a few minutes. And his popularity, though gained by much merit, was lost by no greater crime than that of trusting too much to militia.

8. The Marquis De La Fayette and Baron De Kalb arrived in the United States in the same small vessel, which made the land at North inlet, near Georgetown, about the

middle of June, in the year 1777. They lay in the offing, and seeing a canoe, with two negroes in it, come out of the inlet a fishing, they sent off a boat, which intercepted them. Fortunately they belonged to Capt. Benjamin Huger, who had just arrived at North Island with his family, to spend the summer. The negroes conducted the marquis and baron to their master's house, where he received them with joy, and, it need not be added, with hospitality. Never was a meeting of three more congenial souls. The major afterwards conducted his two illustrious guests to Charleston. Major Huger was the father of Col. Huger, who afterwards engaged in the well known enterprize of delivering the marquis from the dungeon of Olmutz; and perhaps the seeds of that honourable undertaking were sown under his father's roof.

9. Puff. L.N. viii.6.24. Vatt. B.2.C.14. S.214-15.

10. Ibid, B.2.C.13. S.200.

11. Vattel B.2.C.17. S.304. B.3.C.13. S.201.

12. Darkness visible.

13. This Ox swamp is twenty-three miles above Kingstree, another mentioned hereafter, is thirteen miles below.

14. Inland swamps in the lower and middle country are called Bays, from their natural growth, which is the bay tree, a name sufficiently appropriate.

15. Bella, plus quam civilia; bella, nullos habitura triumphos.

16. He was taken from Capt. Ball, at Black Mingo.

17. Notwithstanding the bruit made in history about this defeat of Sumter, the author can re-assert, and from written evidence now before him, that Sumter was in three days at the head of a very respectable force. This was not obtained by any communication from the general, but by an investigation of dates.

18. Chapter II Paragraph 8.—A. L.

19. Marion was often without a surgeon to dress his wounded, and if a wound reached an artery the patient bled to death.

Chapter 3:
Campaign of 1781

The year 1781 commenced under auspices more propitious than those of the last year. The British had exercised so much oppression and rapacity over all those who would not join them, and so much insolence over those who did, and were in the least suspected, that the people of South Carolina found there was no alternative but between a state of downright vassalage and warfare. Most of the men of principle already had, or were prepared to take up arms against the enemy, and in general the unprincipled only remained with them in the expectation of plunder. Their army too, being divided into different cantonments over the country, while it extended their oppression, exposed their weakness. The history of all ages shows that a country may be overrun with more facility than kept in a state of subjection, and that a partisan warfare is the best that can be carried on against an enemy of superior force and discipline.

During the present winter Lord Cornwallis formed a design of conquering the upper counties of North Carolina, and marched by the way of Charlotte towards Salisbury, for that purpose. This part of the country was thickly covered with underwood, and settled by a hardy race of industrious yeomanry, all friends of their country. He was fired upon from behind bushes and fences, trees and rocks, by companies in ambush, and individuals on foot and on horseback, and was so much annoyed that he was obliged to retreat back to Winnsborough. The news of this expedition was industriously spread abroad, and encouraged the people of South Carolina to follow the example. In the mean time, Gen. Gates had been superceded in the command of the southern army by Gen. Greene.

With the character of this leader it is intended to make the reader better acquainted than he has been heretofore. His command begun with a good omen, which in all times has had its effect. In a few hours after his arrival in camp at Charlotte, he received the news that Col. Washington had taken Rugely and one hundred men, by the well known stratagem of mounting a pine log over against his block house, which he mistook for a field piece.[1] Gen. Greene had not only no more than one thousand continentals and about as many militia, but was also bare of ammunition and clothing, and had no money to pay them. With this force he marched down to Pedee, in South Carolina, and took a position near Hick's creek, on the east side of the river, not many miles from Chatham. From this place his first despatch to Gen. Marion is dated, the 19th

Chapter 3: Campaign of 1781

Jan. 1781, in which he says, "by the last accounts, Lieut. Col. Tarleton was in motion, with about one thousand troops, towards Gen. Morgan." On the 23d Jan. Gen. Greene congratulates Marion on Morgan's victory over Tarleton, and writes him the particulars. On the 25th he says, "before this I hope you have received the agreeable news of the defeat of Lieut. Col. Tarleton. After this nothing will appear difficult."

As the defeat of Tarleton at the Cowpens has been related by many American writers, whose works are generally read, the account of the renowned chief himself, who was unexpectedly foiled, and which is now out of print, will be extracted for the amusement of the historical reader. "Near the end of the last year, (1780) information had been received by Lord Cornwallis, that Gen. Greene had made a division of his troops, which did not exceed fourteen hundred men, exclusive of militia, and that he had committed the light infantry and Col. Washington's cavalry to Gen. Morgan, with directions to pass the Catawba and Broad rivers, to collect the militia, and threaten Ninety-Six. It is not to be supposed Gen. Greene would have adopted the hazardous plan of dividing his forces, if he had received information of Gen. Leslie's command being withdrawn from Virginia, and united to the force in South Carolina; because such an accession of strength would produce a movement from Winnsborough (where Cornwallis then lay,) and might separate the two divisions of the American army, and endanger their safety. To attain this object, (the separation of the two divisions of the American army,) Col. Tarleton was now detached from the main army of Lord Cornwallis, and was to be supported by his lordship, and Gen. Leslie as soon as he arrived; with orders to push Morgan to the utmost. Tarleton's force was his corps of cavalry and infantry of five hundred and fifty men; the first battalion of the 71st, of two hundred men; two hundred men of the 7th regiment, new recruits; and fifty dragoons of the 17th regiment—total one thousand men. Morgan retreated before Tarleton till the commanding officer in front of the British reported the American troops were halted and forming. (17th Jan.) Lieut. Col. Tarleton, having obtained a position he certainly might deem advantageous, did not hesitate to undertake the measures his commander and his own judgment recommended. He ordered the legion dragoons to drive in the militia, that Morgan's disposition might be inspected. The American commander had formed a front line of about one thousand militia; his reserve of five hundred continental infantry, one hundred and twenty of Washington's cavalry, and three hundred back woodsmen. Tarleton ordered his infantry to disencumber themselves of every thing except arms and ammunition, to file to the right, till they became equal to the flank of the American front line; the legion infantry were added to their left, and under the fire of a three pounder they were to advance within three hundred yards of the enemy. This situation being acquired, the 7th regiment was commanded to form on the left of the legion infantry, and the other three pounder was given to its right. A captain with fifty dragoons, was placed on each flank. The first battalion of the 71st extended to the left of the 7th, one hundred and fifty yards in the rear, and composed, with two hundred cavalry, the reserve.

"The animation of the officers and soldiers promised assurances of success. The troops moved in as good line as troops could move, at open files. The militia, after a short contest, were dislodged. The British approached the continentals, and the fire on both sides produced much slaughter. The cavalry on the right were ordered to charge the enemy's left, and executed the order with great gallantry, but were driven back by the reserve and Col. Washington's cavalry. As the contest between the British infantry and continentals was equally balanced, Tarleton brought the 71st into line, and ordered a movement in reserve to threaten the enemy's right flank. Upon the advance of the 71st all the infantry again moved on; the continentals and back woodsmen gave ground; the British rushed forwards; an order was despatched to the cavalry to charge; an unexpected fire at this instant from the Americans who came about, stopped the British and threw them into confusion. Exertions to make them advance were useless. The part of the cavalry which had not been engaged, fell likewise into disorder, and an unaccountable panic extended along the whole line. The Americans advanced and augmented their astonishment. A general flight ensued. Neither promises nor threats could gain attention. All attempts to restore order, recollection or courage proved fruitless. Two hundred dragoons forsook their leader, fourteen officers and forty horsemen were, however, not unmindful of their own reputation, or their commanding officer. Col. Washington's cavalry were charged and driven back into the continental infantry by this handful of brave men. Another party who had seized upon the baggage were dispersed, and this detachment retired towards Broad river unmolested. The number of the killed and wounded at the Cowpens, amounted to near three hundred on both sides, officers and men inclusive; this loss was almost equally shared. But the Americans took two pieces of cannon, the colours of the 7th regiment, and near four hundred prisoners." Thus far Col. Tarleton. Gen. Moultrie received his account of this action of the Cowpens "from an officer of great veracity and high rank, who was conspicuous on that day;" supposed to be Col. Washington. The substance of his account shall now be given; that the two may be compared. Gen. Morgan drew up his men in an open pine barren, the militia of about four hundred men, under Col. Pickens, formed the first line. The continentals of about five hundred men, two hundred of whom were raw troops, formed the second line, under Col. Howard, two hundred yards in the rear. Col. Washington, with seventy-five continental cavalry, and forty-five militia under Capt. M'Call, in the rear. Pickens ordered his men to reserve their fire till the enemy came within fifty yards, which they did, and fired with great success; but they were soon obliged to give way and retreat behind the second line, which received them warmly; at length the second line began to give way.

Chapter 3: Campaign of 1781

Col. Washington, perceiving this, rode up to their rear with his cavalry, and told Howard, "if he would rally his men and charge the enemy's line, he would charge the cavalry who were cutting down the militia." His riding so close to the rear stopped the British, and Howard rallied his men in the mean time, and charged with fixed bayonets. Col. Washington charged the cavalry and routed them; the militia at the same time recovered themselves and began to fire, and the whole threw the enemy into the utmost confusion. Howard called out to them, "to lay down their arms and they should have good quarters." Upwards of five hundred men threw down their arms and surrendered. Two hundred were left dead on the field, and a great number wounded. Besides the two field pieces mentioned by Tarleton, six hundred men, eight hundred stand of arms, and thirty-five baggage waggons, fell into the hands of the Americans. Col. Washington pursued the British cavalry twenty-five miles."

By this last account the disparity in numbers was not great, and as one half the Americans were either militia or new levies, the superiority was on the side of Tarleton, whose men, except two hundred, were veterans, and he had two field pieces. The ground too he acknowledges was advantageous; so that every thing was in his favour, but an agency which he could not control. But in the last account we can find no place where he and his handful of brave men could encounter Col. Washington. In his bewildered fancy perhaps it was some other object he encountered, since for the space of five and twenty miles, not their faces, but only their backs were to be seen. The fact is, that never was victory more complete, never was vanity more humbled, nor cruelty more justly requited than in the defeat of this tyrannical man. Its first effect was to raise the spirits of the people; its ultimate consequence was the downfall of Cornwallis and peace to the country. But most severe trials are yet to be surmounted, and patriotism the most exemplary remains yet to be recorded.

On the day the last letter of Greene, of the 23d Jan. was written, Gen. Marion and Col. Lee projected a joint expedition to surprise Georgetown. Capts. Carnes and Rudulph, with ninety men, dropped down the Pedee from Snow's island in a boat, to fall in on the back of the town by Winyaw bay, while Marion and Lee were to come down with the main body by land.—Carnes with his party went ashore at Mitchell's landing, and marched over his rice-field bank into the town at day light. The surprise would have been complete, had they pushed up directly to the redoubt, but they delayed too long on the Bay. They took the commandant, Col. Campbell, out of his bed, and killed Major Irvine and some others; but Marion and Lee could not arrive in time to cooperate. The redoubt was alarmed and placed in a state of defence, and Carnes was obliged to retreat. The great cause of delay was the inclination to take the commandant, by which they lost the fort and the town. Lieut. Cryer killed Irvine, by whose orders he had received five hundred lashes some time before, for attempting to take away his horse from Georgetown.

On the 28th Jan. Gen. Huger transmitted an order from Greene to Marion, to strike at the posts beyond Santee. But this Gen. Marion had anticipated.—From Cordes' plantation, in advance, at the distance of one hundred miles from Greene, and on the 29th Jan. he had detached Col. Postell and Major Postell on this important service. The latter had but thirty-eight men, and it is presumed from circumstances, the colonel had about an equal number. The colonel burnt a great quantity of valuable stores at Manigault's ferry, and the major a great many more in its vicinity.—Thence the latter posted to Keithfield, near Monk's corner, and burnt fourteen waggons loaded with soldiers' clothing, baggage and other valuable stores, and took prisoners about forty British regulars, without losing a man. To the Postells "nothing indeed appeared difficult." They received the thanks of Gen. Greene.

About the beginning of this year, Gen. Marion appointed two aids, Thomas Elliott and Lewis Ogier, the first of whom conducted the most of his correspondence. He formed a mess of which Col. Hugh Horry and Col. James Postell were inmates, and apparently his principal counsellors; Serjt. Davis was his caterer, and supplied his dinners, such as they were: heretofore he had seldom any thing but meat and sweet potatoes, and often not both of these at a time, but now he had the luxury of rice. He did what was of more consequence than this, he put in requisition all the saws in the country, and all the blacksmiths, and made swords for four troops of militia cavalry.—He had so little ammunition this expedient was necessary. He gave the command of this corps to Col. Peter Horry, who had been a captain with him in the second regiment and had been an excellent infantry officer.—His major was Benson, and his captains John Baxter, John Postell, Daniel Conyers and James M'Cauley; John T. Greene soon after succeeded Baxter, who was appointed colonel on the resignation of Ervine. Hugh Horry had command of M'Donald's regiment, who was a prisoner on parole, and his officers have been mentioned. Capt. Wm. M'Cottry commanded a company of riflemen who were the dread of the enemy. As the brigade was not strong enough for this corps of horse to act in conjunction, single troops were commonly detached by the general. At the head of a party of this cavalry Col. Peter Horry had soon an opportunity to make a trial of his skill in cavalry evolutions. He met and charged a troop of British horse on Waccamaw neck, but by his own account he appears to have been rather worsted, for he was unhorsed himself and his life saved by Serjt. M'Donald; however he brought off some prisoners. Major John Postell, who was mentioned before, was stationed to guard the lower part of Pedee, had better fortune. On the 18th Jan. Capt. James Depeyster, with twenty-nine grenadiers of the British army, had posted himself in the dwelling house of the major's father, and Postell commanded but twenty-eight militia men. Towards day on the morning after, the major, by knowing well the ground and avoiding the sentinels, got possession of the kitchen, and summoned Depeyster to

Chapter 3: Campaign of 1781

surrender; this was at first refused, and the major set fire to the kitchen. He then summoned him a second time, with the positive declaration if he did not surrender he would burn the house; the British being intimidated, laid down their arms and surrendered unconditionally.

From a part of the correspondence of Gen. Marion with Capt. Saunders, now commandant of Georgetown, it appears that he had either soon after the 17th Jan. or before that, imprisoned Mr. John Postell, the father of the major; Gen. Marion offers "to exchange him, and hopes humanity will induce Capt. Saunders to treat him like a gentleman."[2] Mr. John Postell was at least seventy years of age, and much afflicted with disease, but possessed the spirit of a Cato.

Soon after this, Col. Peter Horry had a conflict with Major Ganey at White's bridge, near Georgetown, which had a more decisive effect than could have been expected at the time. Early in the morning he made a charge upon a party who were killing beeves at the camp near that place. They fled and were pursued through the woods on the left towards Georgetown, with some disorder on the side of Horry. In the mean time the firing was heard in the town, and their tory friends came out to their assistance. A kind of savage warfare now took place in the woods, between the Sampit and Black river roads, during the whole morning. A party of Horry's was at one time seen advancing, and the tories retreating; then again the tories were advancing, and a party of Horry's retreating. At one time the commander was left as he thought alone, and Capt. Lewis at the head of a party was rushing on to shoot him down, when suddenly from behind a tree off went the gun of a boy by the name of Gwyn, and shot Lewis, whose party thinking more guns were behind trees ran away. As Lewis fell his gun went off and killed Horry's horse. Finally the tories were routed. In this affair Serjt. M'Donald performed essential service; he had singled out Ganey as his object of attack, and the latter fled from him.—In going at full speed down the Black river road, at the corner of Richmond fence, M'Donald shot one of Ganey's men, and overtaking him soon after thrust a bayonet up to the hilt in his back; the bayonet separated from the gun, and Ganey carried it into Georgetown; he recovered, but tired of a garrison life, after a few months he and his men deserted the British.

As the navigation of the Wateree river was at that time imperfect, the British were obliged to have most of their stores of rum, salt, ammunition and clothing sent over land, across Nelson's ferry, to Camden, and as the Americans were destitute of these articles, constant conflicts took place upon that road to obtain them from the enemy. To secure these, they had established a line of posts, at Biggen, at Nelson's, and at Scott's lake. Besides this protection, their supplies were always attended by escorts, which, since the enterprizes of the two Postells, seldom consisted of less than three or four hundred men. About the middle of February, Major M'Ilraith was marching from Nelson's ferry at the head of one of these escorts, and Marion with about an equal force assailed him near Halfway swamp, on the road; he first cut off two pickets in his rear in succession, then wheeling round his main body, attacked him in flank and in front. As M'Ilraith had no cavalry, his situation became perilous in the extreme. By a forced march, and constant skirmishing, he at length gained a field upon the road, now belonging to Mr. Matthew James; and as it was open and enclosed, he posted himself on the west of the road, within the enclosure. On the east, skirting the road, there is a large cypress pond stretching towards Halfway swamp, and on the verge of this Marion pitched his camp. Here M'Ilraith sent him a flag, reproaching him with shooting his pickets, contrary, as he alleged, to all the laws of civilized warfare, and defying him to a combat in the open field. Marion replied, that the practice of the British in burning the houses of all who would not submit and join them, was more indefensible than that of shooting pickets, and that as long as they persisted in the one he would persevere in the other. That as to his defiance, he considered it that of a man in desperate circumstances; but if he wished to witness a combat between twenty picked men on each side, he was ready to gratify him. The offer was accepted, and a place pitched upon to the south of an oak tree, which still stands in the field. Accordingly, Gen. Marion appointed Maj. John Vanderhorst, then a supernumerary officer, to take command of this band, and Capt. Samuel Price, of All Saints, to be second in command. The names of the men were written on slips of paper, and presented to them individually, and the first slip was handed to Gavin Witherspoon. Not one refused. Vanderhorst formed in Indian file, and they proceeded to the fence, where Gen. Marion met and harangued them to the following effect: "My brave soldiers! you are twenty men picked this day out of my whole brigade. I know you all, and have often witnessed your bravery. In the name of your country, I call upon you once more to show it. My confidence in you is great, and I am sure it will not be disappointed. Fight like men, fight as you have always done, and you are sure of the victory." This short speech was received with applause by the combatants. Vanderhorst now asked Witherspoon, "What distance would you choose as the surest to strike with buck shot?" "Fifty yards for the first fire," was the reply. Then, said the commander, "when we get within fifty yards, my boys, as I am not a good judge of distances, Mr. Witherspoon will tap me on the shoulder. I will then give the word, and you will form on my left opposite those fellows. As you form, each man will fire at the one directly opposite him, and my word for it, few will be left for a second shot." The British had now formed in a single line in front of the oak, and Vanderhorst advanced boldly on within one hundred yards. At this juncture, an officer was seen to pass swiftly on toward the oak, and the enemy shouldered their muskets and retreated with a quick step towards the main body. Vanderhorst and his men gave them three huzzas! but did not at that distance fire a shot. Thus a British officer was met on his own boasted ground and proved recreant. The next

Chapter 3: Campaign of 1781

morning Major M'Ilraith abandoned his heavy baggage, left his fires burning, and retired silently from the ground, along the river road towards Singelton's mill, distant ten miles. Near day Marion discovered his movement, and detached Col. Hugh Horry with one hundred men to get ahead of him, before he should reach the mill. The colonel made all possible speed, but finding he could not overtake him, detached Major James at the head of a party mounted on the swiftest horses, to cross the mill pond above, and take possession of Singelton's houses, which stood on a high hill, commanding a narrow defile on the road, between the hill and Wateree swamp. Major James reached the houses as the British advanced to the foot of the hill; but found Singelton's family down with the small pox. This was more dreaded than the enemy. He gave them one fire, by which a captain was killed, and retired. As M'Ilraith was now in a strong hold, Marion pursued him no further.

The character of Major M'Ilraith has been constantly represented by the inhabitants of this state, among whom he passed as the most humane of all the officers of the British army. To those in their power even forbearance was at that time a virtue, but his virtues were active. It has been currently reported that he carried his dislike to house burning so far, that he neglected to carry into effect the orders of his commander in chief on that point to such an extent, as to gain his ill will and that of many other British officers.—How much it is to be regretted that the rigid rules of warfare should have arrayed such a man in opposition to Marion, when both professed the same humane principles.

We come now to the most interesting part of the warfare of Gen. Marion, which, bringing into action all the energies of his officers and men, at the same time developed all the skill and patience of their commander.

At the juncture of the retreat of Gen. Greene before Cornwallis, Sumter and Marion were left alone in South Carolina; Sumter on the Catawba, in York district, and Marion on the Pedee, at Snow's island, about two hundred miles apart, and Lord Rawdon directly between them, with a much superior force. Thus situated his lordship laid a well digested plan to crush Marion. Col. Watson with a British regiment, and Harrison's regiment of tories, amounting in the whole to more than five hundred men, was ordered to march down the Santee, towards Snow's island; and he commenced his expedition from Fort Watson about the first of March.

Shortly after Col. Doyle with another British regiment, was directed to proceed by the way of M'Callum's ferry on Lynch's creek, and down Jeffer's creek, to the Pedee road to the same point, where they were to form a junction. Doyle had to open a road from M'Callum's to Pedee, and his approach, though slow, was unexpected; but Marion's scouts placed from Camden down, with relays of horses, soon informed him of Watson's movement. By one of his rapid marches he met him at Wiboo, about midway between Nelson's and Murray's ferry, and at this swamp commenced his arduous contest with Watson. Col.

Peter Horry was placed in advance at the swamp, while the general with the cavalry, and remainder of the brigade, amounting to about four hundred men, lay in reserve. Horry made considerable impression upon the tories in advance; but Watson with two field pieces, and at the head of his column of regulars, dislodged him from the swamp, and the tory cavalry under Harrison pursued. As they advanced, Gavin James, a private of gigantic size and spirit, mounted on a strong grey horse, and armed with a musket and bayonet, threw himself in their way. He first deliberately fired upon the column and one man fell. The causeway was narrow and this occasioned a pause, in which a volley was fired at him without effect. One dragoon advanced and was struck off his horse by the bayonet. A second came to his aid and shared a like fate; in falling he laid hold of the musket near the muzzle to jerk it away, and James dragged him forty or fifty paces. This bold action produced a considerable effect, and was soon followed by many others, not so well recollected, and too numerous to be inserted.—Harrison had not pursued far, when Marion ordered the cavalry to charge; Capts. M'Cauley and Conyers, met him, and soon dispersed his force; whilst Conyers killed one of his officers, said to be Major Harrison, with his own hands. Thus were the tories intimidated at the outset.

On the 9th of March, Col. Watson encamped at Cantey's plantation, and wrote a letter to Gen. Marion, in which he justifies (what the other had complained of by a previous communication,)[3] the burning of houses and the hanging of those citizens who had taken paroles, and afterwards joined the Americans, upon the principles of the laws of war and nations.—It seems the colonel had reference to the code of barbarous nations. Marion made him no reply, but gave orders to his nightly patroles, to shoot his sentinels and cut off his pickets. Such a retaliation was to be expected; and thus raged the civil warfare.

Watson marched down the river, and at Mount Hope had to build up the bridges, and to sustain a second conflict with Col. Hugh Horry, at the head of Marion's advance. By dint of his field pieces, and the strength of his column, he at length made good his way. Near Murray's ferry he passed the Kingstree road to his left, and when he came to the Black river road, which crosses at the lower bridge, he made a feint of still continuing down the Santee; but soon after wheeling took that road on which the lower bridge was, distant twelve miles. His manoeuvre did not long deceive Marion. He detached Major James at the head of seventy men, thirty of whom were riflemen under M'Cottry, to destroy the remnant of the bridge, which had been partially broken, and to take post there, while the general kept an eye on Watson.

The pass of the lower bridge was now to decide the fate of Williamsburgh, and seventy of her sons, under her most approved leaders, were gone forth to defend it. Maj. James proceeded with great expedition, and crossing the river by a shorter route than the road, arrived at the bridge in time to throw down

Chapter 3: Campaign of 1781

two of the middle arches, and to fire the string pieces at the eastern end. At this place the west bank of the river is considerably elevated, the east low and somewhat swampy, and on the west the road passes to the bridge through a ravine; the river is forty or fifty yards wide, and though deep, was fordable below the bridge. As soon as the breach in it was effected, Maj. James drew up M'Cottry's riflemen on each side of the ford and end of the bridge, so as to have a fair view of the ravine, and disposed the rest of his little band on the flanks. Not long after, Marion arriving, took post in the rear, and sent Capt. Thomas Potts, with his Pedee company, to reinforce Maj. James; and this had scarcely been effected, when Watson's field pieces opened their fire, from the opposite bank to clear his way, for a passage at the ford. These field pieces could not be brought to bear on the low grounds to the east without exposing his artillerists on the hill to the fire of the riflemen. His balls hit the pines across the river, about midway their trunks, or passed over disregarded. This attempt not succeeding, Watson drew up his columns in the old field over the river, and his advance was now seen approaching the ford with an officer at its head, waving his sword. M'Cottry fired the signal gun, and the officer clapped his hand to his breast and fell to the ground. The riflemen and musketeers next poured in a well directed and deadly fire, and the British advance fled in disorder; nor did the reserve move forward to its support. Four men returned to bear off their officer, but all four shared his fate. In the evening, Watson succeeded in removing his dead and wounded, and took up his head quarters at John Witherspoon's, a mile above the bridge. Here he was overheard to say, "that he never saw such shooting in his life." To men fighting for their homes, wives, families, and their very existence, "nothing appeared difficult;" and good shooting, if not a virtue in them, was highly commendable. Gen. Marion took a position on a ridge below the ford of the river, which is still called the general's island. Next day he pushed M'Cottry and Conyers over the river, and recommenced shooting Watson's pickets and sentinels. Watson posted himself a little farther up the river, at Blakely's plantation, where he pitched his camp in the most open place he could find, but still Marion kept him in a bad humour, (as his letters from that place indicate,) and his regulars in a constant panic. Here he remained for more than a week[4] in inactivity and irresolution; perhaps he waited for Doyle to make an impression at Snow's island; but if Marion heard of Doyle, he kept it a profound secret. While Blakely's and Witherspoon's provisions lasted, his present plan answered pretty well; but when they failed, it became necessary to have more at a greater distance, and these could not be obtained, but by daily skirmishes. In these Capt. Conyers was greatly distinguished. He was most daring, and sat and managed his horse so remarkably well, that as was the case with the centaur of old, they might have been taken for one animal. Conyers was at this time fighting under the auspicious eye of a young lady,[5] to whom his faith had been plighted, and beneath her alternate smiles and fears, he presented himself daily before the lines of the enemy, either as a single champion, or at the head of his troop. Often did she hear them repeat, "Take care! there is Capt. Conyers!" It was a ray of chivalry athwart the gloom of unrelenting warfare.

To increase the panic of the British, Serjt. M'Donald, with a rifle, shot Lieut. Torriano through the knee, at the distance of three hundred yards. This appears to have softened even the proud spirit of Watson; for, on the 15th of March, he wrote a letter to Marion, stating, "we have an officer and some men wounded, whom I should be glad to send where they could be better taken care of. I wish, therefore, to know if they will be permitted to pass to Charleston." Gen. Marion wrote for a list of them, and next day sent the following pass: "Gen. Marion's pass, granted to Lieut. Torriano and twelve privates.—One officer and six wounded men, with six attendants, of the British troops, are permitted to pass to Nelson's ferry, thence to Charleston, unmolested," &c. Col. Watson was now literally besieged; his supplies were cut off on all sides, and so many of his men killed, that, he is said by tradition, to have sunk them in Black river to hide their number. There is a quarry of rock in the neighbourhood of the place, and the only one in that part of the country, where, it is said, he sunk his men. At length Watson, decamping, made a forced march down the Georgetown road; but paused at Ox swamp, six miles below the lower bridge. On each side of the road there was then a thick, boggy swamp—trees were felled across the causeway—three bridges were destroyed, and Marion was watching him with the eye of an eagle. Thus situated, and having to force a more difficult pass at Johnson's swamp, ten miles ahead, Watson most prudently wheeled to the right, and passed on, through open piney woods, to the Santee road, distant about fifteen miles. When overtaken by Marion upon this road, his infantry were passing like horses at a full trot. Here he had not so many obstacles to encounter as on the other road, and, by wheeling covertly and marching so briskly, had gained considerable ground. However, Col. Peter Horry now advanced ahead with the cavalry and riflemen, and annoyed him in flank and in front, while Marion attacked in the rear, until they reached Sampit bridge, where the last skirmish took place. News from Doyle appears to have arrested Marion's progress, and summoned him to new perils.

Watson reached Georgetown, with two waggon loads of wounded men.[6] It is evident from an intercepted letter of his of the 20th of March, that he had been hemmed in so closely that he was in want of every thing, and had taken this route to Georgetown, fifty miles out of his way, to obtain supplies. From Fort Watson to the lower bridge, he had not advanced more than forty miles on his premeditated route to join Doyle.

In the mean time, Col. Doyle, an active, enterprising officer, had driven Col. Ervin, who commanded only a weak guard, from Snow's island. But

Chapter 3: Campaign of 1781

before retreating he had Marion's arms, stores and ammunition thrown into Lynch's creek. This, at the crisis, was a most serious loss.

From Sampit, Gen. Marion marched back towards Snow's island; on the way he received intelligence that Doyle lay at Witherspoon's ferry, and he proceeded forthwith to attack him. Doyle had taken a position on the north side of the ferry, and when M'Cottry, in advance, with his mounted riflemen, arrived at the creek, the British were scuttling a ferry boat on the opposite side. He took a position behind trees, and gave them a well directed and deadly fire; they ran to their arms and returned a prodigious volley, which did no more harm than that of knocking off the limbs of trees among the riflemen. Doyle had received news, which occasioned him to retreat for Camden. The ferry boat being now scuttled and sunk on the opposite side, and Lynch's creek being swollen, and at this place wide and deep, Gen. Marion proceeded up the creek, and swam over it at the first place he reached, five miles above Witherspoon's. This was the shortest route to come at Doyle. He pursued all that day, and the next morning till nine or ten o'clock, when he came to a house where Doyle had destroyed all his heavy baggage, and had proceeded on with great celerity towards Camden. This seemed mysterious at the time; but here Marion halted.

It appears from what follows, shortly, as well as from Horry's account, that this pursuit was undertaken by Gen. Marion with the desperate resolution of either selling his own life and that of his followers, as dearly as possible, or of cutting his way through the enemy to make good a retreat into North Carolina. Happily for his country, Doyle evaded him, and thus prevented the dangerous attempt. The general now received the melancholy account of the extent of his loss in ammunition and other stores on Snow's island, which under present circumstances appeared irretrievable. However he was but little disposed to brood over misfortunes, and if he had, his enemies were not inclined to allow him leisure. In the mean time Col. Watson, having refreshed and reinforced his party, and received a fresh supply of military stores and provisions at Georgetown, proceeded again towards the Pedee. On his march he had nothing to impede him but a few bridges broken down. He took the nearest route across Black river at Wragg's ferry, and crossing the Pedee at Euhany, and the little Pedee at Potato bed ferry, he halted at Catfish creek, a mile from where Marion court house now stands.—Here Ganey's party flocked in to him in such numbers that he was soon nine hundred strong. Gen. Marion returning from the pursuit of Doyle, and hearing of the approach of Watson, crossed the Pedee and encamped at the Warhees, five miles from him. At this place he consulted with his field officers then in camp, and informed them that although his force was now recruited to five hundred men, that yet he had no more ammunition than about two rounds to each man, and asked them "if he should retreat into the upper parts of North Carolina, or if necessary to the mountains, whether they would follow him." With a firm and unanimous voice the resolution to follow him was adopted. These field officers, whose names should be engraved on tablets of brass, were Cols. Peter Horry, Hugh Horry, James Postell and John Ervin, and Majors John James, John Baxter and Alexander Swinton.

Not long after this resolution was taken, Gen. Marion met Capt. Gavin Witherspoon, who said to him, "General had we not better fight Col. Watson before any more tories join him." "My friend," replied he, "I know that would be best, but we have not ammunition." "Why, general," said Witherspoon, "here is my powder horn full," holding it up. "Ah! my friend," said Marion, "you are an extraordinary soldier, but as for others, there are not two rounds to a man." Witherspoon passed off in silent sorrow; but as soon as he reached his camp, met Baker Johnson, an old tried whig, who begged him for God's sake to give him something to eat, and he set before him some cold rice in a pot. While Johnson was eating, Witherspoon sat pondering over what he had heard for some time; but at last inquired, "What news, Johnson?" "Fine news," said he, "I saw a great number of continental troops, horse and foot, crossing at Long bluff." "Come and tell the general," said Witherspoon. "No," replied the other, "I am starving with hunger, and if the general wants the news he must come to me." Witherspoon immediately posted off to the general, who lost no time in going to Johnson; around whom some hundreds were soon collected. The bearer of the good tidings was to be depended on. The news was sudden and unexpected, and to men now in a state of desperation nothing could be more transporting. Scarce was there an eye but what was suffused with tears of joy. All sufferings appeared now to be at an end, and that balm of the soul hope began to revive. But while Johnson was still communicating his intelligence, it was confirmed by the sound of a drum in the rear; and soon after by the arrival of Major Conyers and Capt. Irby, with Lieut. Col. Lee's legionary infantry. By Conyers, Marion received orders from Gen. Greene to join Lee, and cooperate with him in striking at the posts below Camden, and in furnishing provisions for the main army;[7] and Lee had moved on towards the Santee for that purpose. Commencing his march immediately, Gen. Marion crossed the Pedee in his rear, and left Witherspoon with a small party to watch Watson. The line of march was directed through Williamsburgh; and Marion joined Lee near Fort Watson, on Scott's lake.

About the same time, Capt. John Brockington, of the tories, had been up to his plantation at Cashway, and hearing the same news with Baker Johnson, pushed over the river, and gave Watson the like information. He lost no time, but immediately rolled his two field pieces into Catfish creek, destroyed all his heavy baggage, re-crossed the little Pedee, and not venturing by Euhany, he passed the Waccamaw at Greene's ferry, and retreating through the neck, between that river and the sea, crossed Winyaw bay, three miles wide, and thus arrived in Georgetown. To those unacquainted with this route, a bare

Chapter 3: Campaign of 1781

inspection of the map of the country will at once give information, how much Marion was dreaded by Watson.

Upon forming a junction with Col. Lee, it was decidedly the opinion of Gen. Marion, that they should pursue Watson, and either take him or prevent his junction with Lord Rawdon. But Lee was of opinion it would lead them too far from Gen. Greene. Gen. Marion must have given up his point with much reluctance, for he was afterwards heard repeatedly to regret that his orders did not permit him to pursue Col. Watson. But, perhaps the true reason was that Marion and Lee were both bare of ammunition, and could get it only by taking Fort Watson. It was left without the presence of its commander, and as in that day there was no road from Kingstree up Black river to Camden, and the swamps were impassable except to hunters, by taking a position at Scott's lake, they would be on the only road there was from Georgetown, on a direct line, to intercept Watson, as he marched up to Camden.—But while Gen. Marion passed through Williamsburgh, his men having now performed a tour of duty of more than a month against Watson, which with all its watchings and privations was unusually severe, and being suddenly relieved from that pressure, many of them took the liberty of going home to recruit themselves; and he was left to his great mortification with only eighty men. However, they soon dropped in, one or two at a time.[8]

On the 15th of April, Gen. Marion invested Fort Watson, at Scott's lake, without any other means of annoyance than musketry. The fort stood on an Indian mound, about forty feet high, and was stockaded, and had three rows of abbatis round it.[9] The besiegers took post between the fort and the lake, to cut off the water; but the besieged sunk a well in the fort. As there were no trees or other covering near the fort, Marion's riflemen were too much exposed at first to fire with effect; but Col. Maham contrived to raise a tower of logs in one night, so high that it overtopped the fort, and the marksmen began to fire into it. Gen. Marion had no entrenching tools to make a regular approach, but on the day after the investment, a party of militia under Ensign Baker Johnson, and of continentals under Mr. Lee, a volunteer in the legion, with a sudden movement, and much intrepidity, made a lodgment near the stockade, and began to pull away the abbatis and fling them down the mound. Lieut. M'Kay, who commanded, then hoisted a white flag, and the garrison, consisting of one hundred and fourteen men and officers, capitulated. Major Eaton had been detached by Gen. Greene, with one field piece, to join Marion, but arrived too late to participate in this siege. The loss of the Americans was only two militia men killed, and three continentals and three militia wounded.—As this fort lay on the great line of communication between Camden and Charleston, its fall was a great loss to the enemy; and by taking it Gen. Marion obtained supplies of ammunition, which he soon turned to great advantage.

During the siege, Col. Watson evaded Marion and Lee. Having arrived in Georgetown, and not yet recovered from his panic, he crossed the north and south Santee, at the lower ferries, and having surmounted this difficulty, he marched up the west side of the river and arrived in Camden by the way of the ferry near the town, with forces much impaired by the incessant attacks of Marion, and long marches, combined with much desertion; but his loss is not confessed by the enemy, nor could it be discovered by the Americans.— Had he been able to have cooperated with Doyle in sufficient time, with their overwhelming force, assisted by Harrison and Ganey, with an equal, if not greater number of tories; there can be little doubt, but Gen. Marion with his scanty means of defence, must either have fallen in the conflict or been driven out of the country. When he first marched from Scott's lake, Col. Watson had only seventy miles to traverse, and only Black river to pass, before he reached Snow's island; yet such was the consummate skill and indefatigable exertions of Gen. Marion, that from the 9th of March until the 10th of April, he had not reached his place of destination, and then made a hasty retreat through roads unfrequented, and over wide swamps and rivers, unpursued. To effect this he took a circuitous route, nearly one hundred miles out of his way, which detained him until about the 9th of May, more than two months from his first setting out on this expedition.

Col. Watson was considered by the British one of their best partisans; yet we have seen how he was foiled. Had his regiment attempted, as was no doubt intended, to ford the river at the lower bridge, they would have found the passage narrow, and the river at that time deep; or had he undertaken to repair the bridge, in either case he must have lost a great portion of his men. He was, however, a better officer than historian or civilian, otherwise he would not have justified the practice of burning houses, in the face of the universal censure cast upon Lewis XIV. for adopting the same measure in the Palatinate. But when Watson, Balfour, and other British officers, professing to know the laws of war and nations, burnt houses and hanged those citizens who had taken deceptive paroles upon their authority, certainly it may be affirmed that Marion, who was self-taught, and had no book of the law of nations, or perhaps any other book in his camp, was justifiable as a matter of retaliation, to shoot down their pickets and cut off their sentinels wherever he could find them; and always to fight such invaders in their own barbarian manner. Nothing ever showed, in such a strong light, the plain good sense of Marion. Col. Watson had orders to burn houses, but did not however appear to wish to carry them rigourously into effect. It is believed he burnt but two; one was the house of Lieut. Dickson, who was with Marion; the other belonged to Nathaniel Dwight, of Waccamaw neck. Upon a retrospection, Col. Watson's character appears in a favourable point of view; and, as far as was consistent with orders, his humanity is undoubted.

Chapter 3: Campaign of 1781

On the 18th of April, Col. William Harden, acting under the orders of Marion, took the British fort at Pocotaligo, with one militia colonel, one major, three captains, three lieutenants, sixty privates and twenty-two dragoons, prisoners. He writes, "I wish you would send some commissions, with your orders. It seems they wait for Col. Hayne, and he says he cannot act without a commission, and I am sure, if he turns out, at least two hundred will join him. If so, I am very certain that this part of the country may be held." Every one has either read or heard of the subsequent melancholy fate of Col. Hayne; but more of that in the sequel.

Major John Postell had been pitched upon as the first victim. After distinguishing himself, as related, he obtained leave from his general to go with a flag to Georgetown, to obtain the release of his father, (who was still a prisoner) and of some others. Capt. Saunders, now the commandant, detained him, and threw him also into gaol, on the plea of his having broken his parole;[10] and, in a long correspondence with Gen. Marion, he and Col. Balfour, the commandant of Charleston, vindicated the measure, as consistent with the laws of war and nations. It appears Balfour was the civilian of the British while here in power. He was just such a minion as would have suited the purposes of Tiberius Caesar. He had several hundreds of Americans pining in want and misery in loathsome prison-ships, and in dungeons under the Exchange, damp and noisome, which he called his provost.

He writes thus to Saunders, concerning Major Postell, "send him by water," (by land was not safe) "by a fast sailer—under a guard—be so good as to let him have no chance of escaping." Be so good here, meant to clap him in irons. This royal tiger, secure in his jungle, was now crouching to spring upon what he deemed defenceless prey; but, while reasoning about the law of nations, Saunders had the folly to send out Capt. Merrett with a flag. Marion immediately detained him, and swore a bitter oath, that if they touched a hair of Postell's head he would hang Merrett. Major Postell lost all further opportunity of distinguishing himself, and underwent a long and rigourous imprisonment; but this had become a common case, and the British knew Marion too well to carry matters further. On the 25th of April,[11] Gen. Greene lay at Hobkirk hill, at that time a mile out of Camden, but now partly in the town. His army consisted of only about seven hundred continentals, and as many militia; his left rested on Pinetree creek, and his right extended across the road leading to Lancaster, uncovered by any obstructions. Having just received a comfortable supply of provisions, which they much wanted, his men were employed in cooking and washing. At this juncture, Rawdon sallied out of Camden, at the head of nine hundred men, his whole disposable force. Between him and Greene, along Pinetree creek, were thick woods and shrubbery, and he preferred this route for concealment. His advance was not suspected, until he was fired upon by the American pickets; but these received him bravely, and during the contest with them, Greene formed his army. The Virginia brigade, under Gen. Huger, took the right; the Maryland brigade, under Col. Williams, the left. The continentals were thus disposed in one line, and the artillery, under Col. Harrison, were in the centre. The reserve were the cavalry, under Col. Washington, and two hundred and fifty North Carolina militia, under Col. Reade. Rawdon advanced with the King's American regiment on the right, the New York volunteers in the centre, and the 63d on the left; his right supported by Robertson's corps, and his left by the volunteers of Ireland. Greene discovering his narrow front, ordered Col. Campbell, of the Virginia, and Col. Ford, of the Maryland line, to turn his flanks; the centre regiments to advance with fixed bayonets, and Washington to gain his rear. Rawdon perceiving his danger, brought up the volunteers of Ireland into line. The battle opened with vigour, and Huger evidently gained ground. Washington in the rear, was carrying all before him, and Col. Hawes in the centre, was descending the hill with fixed bayonets. At this flattering moment, the veteran regiment of Gunby, the 1st Maryland, fired contrary to orders; while Capt. Armstrong, with two sections, was moving ahead upon the enemy. Gunby, being anxious to lead his regiment into battle thoroughly compacted, ordered Armstrong back, instead of making him the point of view in forming. Retrograde being the consequence of this order, the British shouted and pressed forward, and the regiment of Gunby, considered the bulwark of the army, never recovered from its panic. Williams, Gunby, and Howard, all strove in vain to bring it to order. The Virginia brigade and second Maryland regiment maintained the contest bravely; but the 2d Maryland, feeling the effect of the retreat of the 1st, became somewhat deranged, and its commander, Lieut. Col. Ford, being wounded in repressing it, this corps also fell back. Rawdon's right having now gained the summit, and flanking Hawes, Gen. Greene ordered a retreat, which was covered by Hawes. Col. Washington having gained his point of attack, and taken two hundred prisoners, was confident of victory; but seeing the retreat, he paroled the officers on the field, and relinquished all the prisoners but fifty. These he brought off, and made good his retreat, with the loss of only three men. Greene's field pieces were now likely to fall into the hands of the enemy, and seeing Capt. John Smith,[12] with his company of picked light infantry, marching off the field in good order, he rode up and called to him, "Smith, my brave fellow, save the field pieces." He immediately fell in the rear, and executed his orders, with the loss of his whole company. All were killed but one man and Smith, and they were made prisoners. Gen. Greene rallied his army at the pass of Sanders' creek, six miles from Camden, and soon after occupied the position Gates had intended to take, at Gum swamp. The British lost between sixty and seventy, and Greene two hundred men. This affair shows upon how small an incident the fate of war generally depends.

Chapter 3: Campaign of 1781

Upon Watson's arrival in Camden, Lord Rawdon being now reinforced, marched out to attack Gen. Greene, at Sawney's creek, on the west side of the Wateree. Greene did not like his position for a general engagement, and took a new one at Cornal's creek, leaving the horse, light infantry and pickets, at his old encampment. The enemy approached and drew up on the opposite side of the creek, but did not attempt to cross; and retired into Camden before night. Early in the morning of the next day (10th of May, 1781,) Lord Rawdon burnt the mill at Camden, the gaol, his stores, and many private houses, and evacuating it, retreated towards Nelson's ferry. Thus was Camden evacuated in less than a year after the British obtained possession of it; but during that short period it had become the scene of innumerable spoliations, and other atrocities. While they held it, the loss of property, and being reduced to poverty, were the least considerable incidents, which happened to the inhabitants. To form an accurate idea, as well of the wretched situation of the people of that town and its vicinity, during this period, as to elucidate a part of history not yet explained, let the reader take the following narrative, partly in and partly out of its due order. Gen. Greene, having traversed that part of North Carolina from Guilford to Pedee, and passed through nearly one half the breadth of South Carolina, by the way of Cheraw hill, and Lynch's creek, arrived at Town creek, four miles below Camden, about the middle of April. Except at the Pedee, the country through which he had marched was destitute of provisions, and no where, unless he had impressed salt provisions, could he find any thing better than beef driven out of the woods; which in April is well known to be lean and nauseating. For the last fifty miles, his route had been across the sand hills, between Pedee and the Wateree; here his guide deserted him, and when he arrived at Town creek, he and his men were at a loss which way to proceed, and were literally starving. The fine low grounds of the Wateree now lay before him, where he expected an abundance of provisions, but he was most grievously disappointed. The British had swept away every thing of the kind that could be found, and what little subsistence was left to the planters was hid in small parcels, and in different places in the swamps. Scarcely any thing fit to eat, was visible, where prior to this period, and subsequently, every kind of provisions had been so abundant. But Gen. Greene, in his distress, happily[13] met with a young man, whom, while he had been at Hick's creek in January last, he had appointed assistant commissary general; and who had served him with zeal and ability in that department. This young man, (the present Gen. Cantey, of Camden,) had but just returned from Dan river, where he had supplied Gen. Greene, with fifteen waggon loads of flour, and nearly one thousand head of hogs, which he had driven from the Pedee, by private ways, with so much skill and address, as to avoid Lord Cornwallis, and the numerous tories by whom he was surrounded; and Cantey was still zealous to serve his country. After gaining some intelligence of the enemy, Gen. Greene requested his commissary to endeavour to get them some provisions, for they were famishing. Cantey's father lived not far off, and recollecting he had some bacon and corn meal hid in a swamp, he immediately went and brought enough for the general's mess, and in a short time after, drove in beeves, such as they were, sufficient for a supper for the men; but so destitute was the neighbourhood, that Cantey recommended it to Gen. Greene to move above Camden, where provisions might be collected from the upper country, and it was more probable he would receive aid from the militia. But for this explanation, the good judgment of Gen. Greene, in taking post above Camden, might well be questioned; since his wisest, and hitherto favoured plan, had been to strike at the posts below. It is thought, if he could have taken a position at Town creek, or Swift creek below, all surprise might have been prevented. At this time, Gen. Greene sent Cantey to Gen. Sumter, distant more than one hundred miles, to request him to join him; but Sumter, who was meditating an attack on fort Granby, declined any further cooperation except in that way. When this answer was communicated to Gen. Greene, by Cantey, he was exceedingly angry, and said he had a great mind to leave them to defend the country as well as they could, without his assistance. Could he have concentrated his force, and had not regarded Ninety-Six, he might have driven the British into Charleston, before the sickly season commenced. But the system of leaving fortresses behind an invading army, so strongly recommended by Machiavelli, and so much followed by Bonaparte, had not yet been adopted in tactics. But we are anticipating our narrative.

Although so weak after the affair at Hobkirk, Gen. Greene, had sent a reinforcement to Marion under Major Eaton with a six-pounder, and on the 8th of May, Marion and Lee commenced firing upon Fort Motte. As soon as Gen. Greene heard of the retreat of Lord Rawdon from Camden, he decamped from Cornal's creek, and moving down on the west bank of the Wateree, took a position near M'Cord's ferry, so as to cover the besiegers. Fort Motte stood on a high hill called Buckhead, a little on the right of the Charleston road, where it leaves the Congaree below M'Cord's. Within its walls was included the house of Mrs. Motte, who had retired to that of her overseer.—When told it was necessary to burn the house, in order to take the fort expeditiously, she at once requested it should be done, and, as the means of effecting it, furnished an Indian bow and arrows. On the night of the 10th, the fires of Lord Rawdon's camp were seen on the Santee hills, in his retreat from Camden, and encouraged the garrison for a while; but on the 12th the house was set on fire, and the commander Lieut. M'Pherson, and one hundred and sixty-five men, surrendered. This deed of Mrs. Motte has been deservedly celebrated. Her intention to sacrifice her valuable property was patriotic; but the house was not burnt, as is stated by historians, nor was it fired by an arrow from an African bow, as sung by the poet.—Nathan Savage, a private in Marion's

Chapter 3: Campaign of 1781

brigade, made up a ball of rosin and brimstone, to which he set fire, slung it on the roof of the house. The British surrendered before much mischief was done to it, and Marion had the fire put out. At the commencement of this siege, Serjt. M'Donald, now advanced to a lieutenancy, was killed. He was a native of Cross creek, in North Carolina, and his father and other relations had espoused the opposite side of the cause. Lieut. Cryer, who had often emulated M'Donald, shared a similar fate. On the 25th Nov. last, we have seen Gen. Sumter severely wounded at Black Stocks; but on the 20th Feb. just three months after, he sat down before Fort Granby, to besiege it, and wrote to Marion, who was his junior officer, to move in such a direction as to attract the attention of Lord Rawdon; but at that time the fort was relieved.

On the same day that Fort Motte surrendered, Gen. Sumter took the British fort at Orangeburgh, with a garrison consisting of seventy tories and twelve British; and in three days after, on the 15th May, he took Fort Granby; long the object of his wishes. This fort was surrendered to him by Major Maxwell, of the British, with nineteen officers, three hundred and twenty-nine men, mostly royalists, and five pieces of ordnance.[14]

Gen. Marion soon after taking Fort Motte, re-crossed the Santee, and encamped at Cantey's plantation, a little more than midway from Nelson's to Murray's ferry, and here he reposed his men for some time and collected reinforcements. In consequence of the evacuation of Camden, and recent successes, the militia turned out well and in high spirits. About the 3d of June, he marched for Georgetown, and appearing before it on the 6th, began his approach by breaking ground; but on the night after the garrison evacuated the town, and took shipping. Remaining here for some time, the general threw off his old habiliments, furnished his wardrobe anew, and fitted himself out with a suit of regimentals. He also procured a couple of mules to transport his baggage. His privations, during the period passed over, were so great that he even wanted a blanket, for on a certain night his bed of pine straw catching fire under him, while he was soundly reposing after one of his forced marches, half of the only one he had was burnt,[15] and his leather cap was wrinkled upon one side, from the contact of the same element. Hereafter he indulged himself with the luxury of coffee for breakfast, but often without bread to it, and he seldom tasted wine or spirits; but was fond of vinegar and water, the drink of a Roman soldier. However, Georgetown was no Capua to him. He soon returned again to Cantey's plantation, and kept out scouts constantly towards Biggen church, where the enemy had a garrison of considerable force.

About this period, Gen. Marion sent Col. Peter Horry with a force to negociate a treaty with Major Ganey and his party. As he could not well turn his arms against him, and the whig settlements on Pedee were left exposed to his depredations, it was good policy to awe him, and to endeavour to keep him quiet. After a little time Horry negociated a treaty, humiliating enough to

Ganey; by which, among other matters, he and his officers agreed to lay down their arms and remain neutral, to deliver up all those who refused to comply with the treaty and all deserters from the Americans, and also to restore all negroes and other plundered property. This treaty was ratified on the 17th of June, but was not strictly complied with until Marion afterwards found leisure to enforce it; as shall be narrated in its place.

Soon after the siege of Fort Motte, Gen. Greene proceeding on with his main army, laid siege to Ninety-Six; in which Lieut. Col. Cruger commanded a garrison of five hundred men, and defended himself with energy and ability. On the right of the besiegers was a strong stockade fort, and on the left a work called the Star redoubt. On the night of the 26th of May, the celebrated Kosciusko, who acted at that time as an engineer for Greene, raised two block batteries within three hundred and fifty yards of the besieged. Soon after a third and a fourth were erected, and lastly a rifle battery within thirty yards of the ditch of the fort. The abbatis was turned, and two trenches and a mine were extended within six feet of the ditch. The fort must soon have been taken; but Lord Rawdon was approaching fast to the relief of the garrison, with two thousand men, which he had lately received from Ireland; (18th June) and Gen. Greene was obliged to raise the siege and retreat over the Saluda. His loss before the fort was about one hundred and fifty men. Lord Rawdon followed the Americans, as far as the Ennoree; but finding the pursuit fruitless, he drew off a part of the garrison from Ninety-Six, and fixed a detachment of his army at the Congaree. Gen. Greene, finding the British force divided, faced about and offered Lord Rawdon battle; but he, in his turn, retreated to Orangeburgh.

About the beginning of July, in this year, Lord Rawdon still lay in Orangeburgh, strongly posted, and Gen. Greene was near, watching his motions. While thus situated, Col. Cruger evacuated his post at Ninety-Six, and marching down through the fork of Edisto, joined Rawdon. As there was no other place at which the Edisto could then be passed but at Orangeburgh, it was out of Greene's power to prevent the junction; and Rawdon's army being thus reinforced, Gen. Greene thought it prudent to retire to Bloom hill, Richardson's plantation, at the High Hills of Santee. Before retiring, however, he detached Gen. Sumter as commander, and ordered Marion to join him, to strike at the posts below. On his way down, Sumter made several successful attacks on British outposts, which were conducted more immediately by Col. Lee and Col. Wade Hampton. Generals Sumter and Marion formed a junction near Biggen, and marched to attack the fort there, garrisoned by five hundred infantry and one hundred cavalry, and commanded by Col. Coates, a spirited officer. His cavalry at first repulsed Sumter's advance, but were driven in by the state troops under Col. Hampton. In the evening after, Col. Coates set fire to the church, which contained all his heavy baggage and stores, and retreating by the Strawberry road over Watboo bridge, destroyed it, and thus gained

Chapter 3: Campaign of 1781

a considerable advance upon Sumter, who had to march round by a ford in pursuit. Coates, in like manner, threw the plank off Huger's bridge, and proceeded rapidly for Quimby. Here he had loosened the planks of the bridge, and was waiting for his rear guard; but, in the mean time, Lee had come up with and taken it. Dr. Irvine, by advancing too far among the combatants, was wounded in this affair,[16] together with several of Lee's men. While Coates was waiting, Capt. Armstrong, at the head of five of his own men, and Capt. James M'Caulay's troop of militia horse crossed the bridge and charged in among the enemy, who at first threw down their arms, but seeing the force so small, soon resumed them, and began to fire; but Armstrong made good his way through them down the road. In the mean while, the passage of the cavalry over the bridge had opened such a chasm[17] in the plank, that Lee could not cross to follow up the advantage thus gained, and the critical moment was lost. The enemy had time to recover from their panic, and to post themselves in Col. Shubrick's house and out houses, which were near. After some delay, Sumter arrived and ordered an attack, which was led on by Marion, whose men, and a regiment of Sumter's, under Col. Thomas Taylor, marched up in open ground, with a view of gaining a fence near the houses; and were exposed to a most galling fire, from riflemen aiming at them from behind cover. More than fifty were killed and wounded, generally of Marion's men, who were most exposed. Capt. Perry and Lieut. June, of his brigade, were killed; and Lieut. Col. John Baxter, who was very conspicuous, from his gigantic size and full uniform, received five wounds; Major Swinton was also severely wounded. A retreat was ordered. The attack was made against Marion's opinion, who blamed Sumter afterwards for wasting the lives of his men. But, with such a force, Sumter had not the disposition to be idle, and wanted only a field piece to have ensured success. Col. Coates had now the command of boats, and a wide river before him, and could easily have effected his retreat in that way to Charleston; but Sumter did not attack him again; because, it was said, a reinforcement was coming to his assistance. After this, Gen. Marion retired to the Santee, and took post at Cordes', and afterwards at Peyre's plantation, near the mouth of the present Santee canal, where he reposed his men and horses, until about the 25th of August.

The British lay near M'Cord's ferry, with a strong party at Monk's corner and Dorchester, and Gen. Greene was still encamped at Richardson's plantation on the High Hills of Santee, directly opposite the enemy, where they might easily see each other; but with a wide swamp between them. About this time Gen. Greene ordered Marion to go to the assistance of Col. Harden, who was then much pressed by the enemy, to the south of the Edisto. Immediately he detached a party of mounted militia under Capt. George Cooper, to the neighbourhood of Dorchester and Monk's corner, to create a diversion there, whilst he with about two hundred picked men, by a circuitous route and forced march of at least one hundred miles, crossed the Edisto, joined Harden and approached the British. When sufficiently near he drew up his men in a swamp upon the road near Parker's ferry, and sent out some of his swiftest horse to lead the British into the ambuscade. While lying there a small party of tories crossed at the ferry, and in passing on one of them called out that he saw a white feather, and fired his gun. This occasioned an exchange of a few shots on both sides; but (as is supposed) it was thought by Major Fraser, who commanded the British, to be only Harden's party that was in the swamp; he pursued the horsemen sent out as a decoy, and led his corps in full charge within forty or fifty yards parallel to the ambuscade. A deadly fire from the swamp, was the first notice he had that a greater force than Harden's was there. He attempted to wheel and charge into the swamp, but only exposed his men the more, as they were thus delayed before the fire, and were wedged up on a causeway so closely that every shot had its utmost effect. Finding all his efforts ineffectual, Fraser at length retreated along the road to the ferry, and thus passed the whole ambuscade. A large body of infantry with a field piece, were now seen advancing, and Marion retreated without counting the dead, but men and horses were seen lying promiscuously in heaps on the road. Although a large body of infantry was advancing, yet Marion in his situation had not much to fear from them, and indeed had often encountered such; therefore the true cause of his retreating could not have been because they were advancing; but the probability is, because he wanted ammunition. How often he was thus impeded in his enterprizes was known only to himself. A party under Capt. Melton, went out the next day to the battle ground, and counted twenty-seven dead horses; the men had been buried. As Marion's men fired with either a ball and buck shot, or heavy buck shot alone, and as none would aim at horses, the loss of the British must have been great.—But though their loss could not be ascertained, the effect of this well conducted affair soon became evident, for at the battle of Eutaw, nine days after, the enemy had but few cavalry in the field. It is not a little surprising that there is no record or date of this action to be found, but in the thanks of congress to Gen. Marion, which fix it on the 31st of August.

In the mean time, Capt. Cooper passed on to the Cypress, and there routed a party of tories, and then proceeding down the road, he drove off the cattle from before the enemy's fort at Dorchester. He next moved on down the Charleston road; a body of tories lay in a brick church, which stood then twelve miles from town; he charged and drove them before him. Next, passing into Goose creek road, he proceeded to the ten mile house, returned and passed over Goose creek bridge, took a circuitous route around the British at Monk's corner and arrived in camp at Peyre's plantation near the canal, where Gen. Marion now lay, with many prisoners, and without the loss of a man. In his letter of the 10th of August, 1781, noted above, Gen. Greene writes to Marion,

Chapter 3: Campaign of 1781

"you will see by Col. Harden's letter, the enemy have hung Col. Hayne; do not take any measure in the matter towards retaliation, for I do not intend to retaliate on the tory officers, but the British. It is my intention to demand the reasons of the colonel's being put to death, and if they are unsatisfactory, as I am sure they will be, and if they refuse to make satisfaction, as I suppose they will, to publish my intentions of giving no quarters to British officers of any rank that fall into our hands. This will be delayed for some few days, to give our friends in St. Augustine[18] time to get off." The measure thus proposed was quite too extensive in its nature to have been carried into effect. The true reason why there was no retaliation was the last, respecting the friends in St. Augustine, and it is suspected that it originated with the governor and council. The British army was now no longer commanded by Lord Rawdon; he had retired to Europe, and was succeeded by Brigadier Gen. Stewart. Lord Rawdon had defended Camden as long as he could with vigour and ability; but lately stained his reputation by the execution of Col. Hayne. In extenuation of this act, it is said by his friends, he only obeyed the orders of his superior; but if he really disapproved that act of cruelty, he could easily have avoided taking a part in it, for as he was shortly to sail for Europe, he might have left the execution of it to Col. Balfour; as being congenial to his natural disposition. This proceeding was sudden and unexpected, and produced a great sensation in the American army. When Gen. Greene demanded the reason of it, Lord Rawdon had either departed or returned no answer; but Balfour stated, that "it took place by the joint order of Lord Rawdon and myself, in consequence of the most express directions of Lord Cornwallis to us, in regard to all those who should be found in arms, after being, at their own request, received as British subjects." Now, although Lord Cornwallis, when flushed with victory, issued cruel orders; yet it is not to be presumed he acted the tyrant so far as to communicate private orders to Rawdon and Balfour; but the only case in which his public orders directed a capital punishment, is the following: "I have ordered in the most positive manner, that every militia man, who has borne arms with us, and afterwards joined the enemy, shall be immediately hanged." But it was never pretended that Col. Hayne had borne arms with the British; when he submitted, he expressly stipulated with Gen. Patterson, that he was not to do so; and when, notwithstanding such stipulation, he was called upon for that service, he positively refused, although threatened with confinement. Besides, both Moultrie and Ramsey assert he did not serve with the British; and as far as negative proof can go, this should be conclusive. But the fact that he bore arms with the British is not charged against him; his accusation was, "being at his own request received as a British subject." Then Col. Hayne neither came within the letter, nor the penalty of the order issued by Lord Cornwallis; and his blood rests upon the heads of Rawdon and Balfour. A fair state of the case is, that Col. Hayne had been considered by the British a character of great influence, and after the fall of Charleston, having applied to Gen. Patterson, then commandant, for a parole, he was refused one, and was threatened with confinement if he would not subscribe a declaration of allegiance. Under the influence of this threat, by the advice of friends, and the stipulation above stated, he was induced to sign the declaration; and he was now tried for a breach of his allegiance. Lord Cornwallis punished for breaches of parole, but this was a new charge, made by Rawdon and Balfour themselves. But Hayne's signature to that instrument, had been obtained by duresse, and the part of the country in which he lived had been for several months in the possession of the Americans, and the British were unable to protect him in his allegiance. These, and no doubt other grounds, might have been alleged in his defence, but he was at first promised, and afterwards refused to be heard by counsel. The law of nations, as we have seen, was often on the lips of Balfour, and here was a case which came clearly within that code. Then the forms of justice should have been carefully observed; the accused should have been heard in his defence; the spirit of the law should have been the guide of the judges, with a leaning in favour of lenity and mercy; the passions ought not to have been suffered to interfere, where the minds of the court should have been regulated by justice and wisdom; and finally, the judges should have proceeded deliberately, avoiding every thing like haste in their decision. Such is the law of nations.[19] But neither the forms of justice, nor the spirit of the law were observed; the accused was tried by a court martial, in which, after the production of the declaration of allegiance, the only inquiry made was, "whether he had been taken in arms?" And that being proved, the defendant received a summary sentence of death. A most feeling intercession was made in his behalf, but in vain; all that could be obtained was a few days delay of the execution, which otherwise would have been hurried on in the most indecent manner. Col. Hayne died, not indeed the death, but with the spirit of a soldier, and a martyr in the cause of civil liberty; he met his fate calmly on the gibbet. The character of Balfour was already so black there was scarcely room for an additional blot; but the execution of Col. Hayne must ever continue a stain upon the reputation of Lord Rawdon. He had not even the excuse that it was the law of the conqueror; for Lord Cornwallis and himself were conquerors no more.

The two hostile armies still lay encamped and watching each other in the positions before mentioned, at Bloomhill and M'Cord's ferry; but about the beginning of September, Gen. Greene, for the want of boats, marched up the Wateree and crossed it not far below Camden,[20] and marching down through the fork between the two rivers, passed the Congaree at Howell's ferry and encamped at Motte's plantation, on a direct route to meet the enemy, who had been encamped but a short distance below him.

Here he received intelligence that the British army commanded by Brigadier Gen. Stewart[21] had retreated and halted at the Eutaw Spring, about forty miles

Chapter 3: Campaign of 1781

below, that they had been reinforced there, and were about to establish a permanent post. To prevent this, he determined to risk a battle, though his force was thought to be inferior. Accordingly he sent back his baggage to Howell's ferry, and proceeded by easy marches to Burdell's plantation seven miles from Eutaw, where he was joined by Gen. Marion. Gen. Stewart had posted himself to great advantage at Eutaw; his head quarters were in a strong brick house, which stood at that time a little to the west of the spring or rather fountain. In his rear, to the south, there was an open field; in his front a thick wood covered with pines and scrubby oaks. Below the fountain on his right there was a deep valley, through which the Eutaw creek, five or six feet deep, takes its course towards the north-east. Between the fountain and the brick house the Congaree road passes to the north.

It was down this road Gen. Greene marched to attack the British army, on the memorable 8th of September, 1781. The effective force of each army was nearly equal, except the cavalry, in which Greene would have had the advantage, if the nature of the ground had permitted the use of it, for none of the ground was then open, and particularly on his left it was covered by scrubby oaks. While moving down the road in the morning with much circumspection, Col. Lee in advance met a party which covered another that was foraging. Several of these were killed, and their captain and forty men taken. Pressing forward, Lee soon met another party, with whom another action commenced, and he requested the support of artillery to counteract that of the enemy, which had now opened. Two field pieces were quickly brought up by Capt. Gaines, and began to fire.

During this firing both armies formed. The South Carolina militia under Marion, and the North Carolina under Col. Malmedy occupied the first line; the South Carolinians on the right. The continentals formed the second line. The Virginians under Col. Campbell, occupied the right. Gen. Sumner with the North Carolina new levied troops, the centre; and the Marylanders, under Cols. Williams and Howard, the left, on the Charleston road. Lee had charge of the right, and Henderson of the left flank, with their cavalry. Two field pieces were disposed in the front and two in the rear line. Washington's horse and Kirkwood's infantry formed the reserve.

The enemy was drawn up in one line, the Buffs on the right, Cruger's corps in the centre, and the 63d and 64th on the left. Major Marjoribanks with one battalion of light infantry was posted on the Eutaw creek, flanking the Buffs, and the cavalry under Major Coffin were drawn up in the open field in the rear; these were not numerous. The artillery were posted on the Charleston road and the one leading to Roach's plantation.—The action commenced about a mile from the fountain. Marion and Pickens continued to advance and fire, but the North Carolina militia broke at the third round.—Sumner with the new raised troops, then occupied their place, and behaved gallantly. Marion's marksmen firing with great precision, and galling the enemy greatly, had now advanced more than half a mile, when the British charged upon them with fixed bayonets, and Marion ordered a retreat. The Virginia and Maryland troops now advanced with trailed arms, and scarcely had Marion cleared the right of the Virginians, when the crash of bayonets was heard. But by degrees it receded, and becoming less and less audible, a loud shout of huzza for America! told the issue of the contest.—Gen. Marion now rallied his men. Col. Henderson of the South Carolina state troops was wounded early in the action, and the command devolved on Col. Wade Hampton, who made a spirited charge; but being warmly received, Col. Washington brought up the reserve to his aid, and at first charged so briskly that the enemy gave way; but advancing into the thickest part of the woods, Marjoribanks came to the assistance of the Buffs; Washington's horse was killed under him, and he was wounded and taken. After this, and the loss of many officers and men, the corps was drawn off by Capt. Parsons. Marjoribanks though victorious on the right, now fell back to assist Stewart; and Major Sheridan with the New York volunteers, threw himself into the brick house. Stewart was busily engaged in rallying his men under cover of the fire from Sheridan; and Greene now ordered Lee to charge upon Coffin. Lee at the beginning of the action had advanced with the legionary infantry upon the left of the enemy, and ordered his cavalry under Eggleston to follow in the rear; but sending for Eggleston, at present, he found that by some mistaken order he had gone to assist Washington. Thus a most favourable opportunity of completing the rout already commenced, was irretrievably lost. Greene had now brought up his artillery against the brick house, and sent for Marion who came to his assistance; but the weight of his metal was too light to effect a breach. Here, after losing many men and making unavailing efforts, he was obliged to desist, bringing off one field piece, which he had taken from the enemy, and losing two of his own. Thus Sheridan and Marjoribanks saved the British army.

 Gen. Greene, in this manner disappointed in the most sanguine expectation of a complete victory, collected all his wounded, except those under the fire of the enemy, and placing a strong picket on the field of battle, retired sullenly from the ground in search of water. The battle had taken place on a dry thirsty soil, and in a hot day, and the want of water was severely felt. Four or five miles up the Congaree road, there is a remarkably boggy pond, still the dread of travellers; the cavalry had passed through it, twice or thrice in the course of the day; and it was now become a filthy puddle; but into this did the men as soon as they arrived, throw themselves headlong, over the shoulders of each other, and drink with an avidity which seemed insatiable. This was the first water in Greene's rear, which is mentioned by historians, as being resorted to by his army.[22] The battle had lasted more than three hours.

Chapter 3: Campaign of 1781

Next morning, Marion and Lee were ordered by a circuitous route to gain the enemy's rear, in order, as it was expected they would retreat, to retard their march and prevent their being reinforced. On the evening of the 9th of September, Stewart piled up the arms of his dead and wounded, and set them on fire, destroyed his stores, left seventy of his own wounded, and some of Greene's, at the Eutaw; and retreated precipitately towards Monk's corner. So hurried was his retreat for fifteen miles, that he brought his first division within a few miles of M'Arthur, coming to his aid, before Marion and Lee reached Ferguson's swamp, their point of destination. To fight between two fires, became hazardous, and the junction of the enemy was effected. Capt. O'Neal of Lee's horse, fell upon the cavalry of their rear guard, and took most of them prisoners; but Stewart continued his retreat to Wantoot, (Ravenel's plantation,) about twenty miles below Eutaw, and Greene pursued to Martin's tavern, fifteen miles. In this battle, the British lost by Greene's account six hundred men, killed and wounded, and five hundred made prisoners. According to Stewart's return, he lost eighty-five killed,[23] three hundred fifty-one wounded, and two hundred fifty-seven missing. The loss of the Americans was five hundred killed and wounded; among whom were sixty officers. The disparity in these returns of the different commanders is great, but Greene's prisoners could be counted at leisure. Lieut. Col. Campbell fell as he was leading the Virginia line to the charge. Gen. Greene says of him, "though he fell with distinguished marks of honour, yet his loss is much to be regretted; he was the great soldier, and the firm patriot." Gen. Marion had many of his men and Col. Hugh Horry wounded; but fewer killed than at Quimby; among the latter was the brave Capt. John Simons, of Pedee.

The British shot generally about five feet too high; but the wind blew that day favourably for Marion's marksmen, and they did great execution. They fired from fifteen to twenty rounds each man. Both sides claimed the victory; but the fruits of one were with the Americans.

It being now autumn, and his men sickly, Gen. Greene retired to the High Hills of Santee, his favourite encampment; Col. Lee calls them, "The benign hills of Santee." At this time Gen. Greene encamped on the range of hills immediately below Stateburgh. His head quarters were at Mr. James', on the right going downwards, a beautiful spot, but now deserted. Many of Greene's wounded officers and men died, and lie buried on a hill near where the author is now writing. An officer, who died of his wound, (Capt. De Wolfe,) lies interred near De Wolfe's spring, on his plantation. He was a most gallant soldier. No mound or grave stone points out the spot where such brave men repose. Even the mounds, where the dead at Eutaw were buried, have been lately violated by the cutting of a ditch through them. Alas! my country, why have such things been suffered?

Marion retired to his favourite encampment, at Peyre's plantation, in Santee river swamp. On the banks of the river at that time there were extensive cornfields on all the plantations, and the most of the low places were cultivated in rice.[24] The crops of three or four years past had been housed, and kept out of the enemy's reach by the difficulty of approach and their retired situation. Here the general fixed himself, much to his liking, in a cane brake, about a quarter of a mile from the river, which however was soon cleared to thatch the huts of himself and his men. Some lakes which skirted the high land, rendered the post difficult of approach, and here was forage for horses, and beef, pork, rice, and green corn[25] for the men, in the greatest abundance. Such a place suited Marion's views exactly, and here, or in the neighbourhood, he encamped often; but did not stay long at present. It appears now there was very little sickness at that day.

Soon after the battle of Eutaw, Gen. Alexander Leslie took command of the British army. On the 17th of September Gen. Greene wrote to Marion: "I have the pleasure to congratulate you on the arrival of Count De Grasse, in Chesapeake bay, with twenty-eight sail of the line, a number of frigates and six thousand land forces; Gen. Washington is also arrived in Virginia to take command of the army. From these circumstances, and from some further intelligence of Lord Cornwallis' movements, it is highly probable that his lordship will endeavour to retreat through North Carolina to Charleston. I must therefore entreat that you will use every exertion to collect a large force of militia together, and as speedy as possible, that we may be able to intercept his lordship." As Gen. Marion's scouts at this time frequently passed round the enemy, and harrassed them much between their camp and Charleston, it has often been a matter of surprise why he should recross the Santee; but this letter explains it, for he crossed it to collect his men, and he encamped at Cantey's plantation a considerable time for that purpose. On the 1st of Sept. Gov. Rutledge had ordered out only the half of the militia; now all were again directed to take the field as formerly.

Another good reason for Gen. Greene and Marion's lying so long inactive at this season, is to be found in a letter in the correspondence mentioned; and though the date is later than the present period, yet the fact comes in properly here. Gen. Marion, as it appears from what follows after, had written to Greene and the governor for ammunition on the 9th of October. On the 10th, Gov. Rutledge answers his letter: "I received yours yesterday, by Mr. Boone, and wrote in the most pressing terms to Col. Williams, (Gen. Greene not being yet returned from Charlotte, for which place he set out on Friday) for a supply of ammunition; I wish to God it was in my power to send you ammunition instantly, but it is not." Col. Otho Williams, who was second in command of the army, writes to Gen. Marion, and, although his letter is not dated, the connection of the correspondence is evident: "As Gen. Greene is not in camp, I took the liberty of opening your letter of the 9th instant. Our stock of ammunition is quite exhausted—we have not an ounce of powder, or a cartridge, in store. The arrival of some military stores which we expect every hour, will put it in the general's power to supply you amply. His excellency Gov. Rutledge has intimated that you meditated an expedition over the Santee; in making your determination, if it is not settled, permit me to recommend to your consideration, that the general depends upon you entirely for intelligence of the enemy's motion." These extracts of letters must be read with astonishment.—With what uncommon fortitude must such men have been endowed, to bear up under such continued discouragements. As Gen. Marion lay a long time here, it will give occasion to relate some other matters, which as fortunate events have for some time past thickened, would have perplexed the narrative to have introduced before.

About the 10th August, Georgetown was burnt.—One Manson, commanding a small armed vessel, arrived within gunshot of the town, and sent a party in a boat under cover of his guns, and set fire to some houses on a wharf at the lower end of the Bay, and the wind favouring, the whole town, except a few houses on the outskirts, was burnt. No doubt Manson had his orders from Balfour.

As the continental troops were without pay and clothing, a plan was adopted by the governor and council to impress all the indigo for public service which could be found, and it was expected that it would now serve instead of money as a medium of exchange. The principle had been authorised by an old militia law, but it was a rigourous measure and a poor expedient, although the best that could be devised at the time. Many thrifty planters had hoarded up their indigo, ever since the commencement of the war, hoping some day to turn it into money. Capt. Wm. Richardson, of Bloomhill, was appointed commissary general by the governor, and assistants were appointed by him in the several districts of the state; who went about with press warrants in their pockets, and parties to assist them, and set a price upon each man's indigo, for which they gave him a receipt, promising payment from the state. The general depot was fixed at Bloomhill.

It was in contemplation at the time likewise to raise two regiments of state troops to be attached to Marion's brigade, and for this purpose all the horses fit for cavalry were impressed, except those of men actually in service. These were indeed high handed measures, but appeared necessary at the time. Winter was approaching, and Gen. Greene states in a letter to Col. Peter Horry, of the 11th of November, "Blankets are so scarce with us, that more than three-fourths of our men are without." A few goods fit for service were afterwards purchased for indigo, but at an enormous advance.[26]

On the 27th of September Gov. Rutledge had ordered by proclamation, that the disaffected should come in within thirty days and do duty for six months.—This measure brought down disgrace, and soon after nearly ruin upon Marion's brigade. This proclamation is long but to the following effect:—

"That whereas, the British had been compelled to evacuate all their strong posts, and could no more give protection to their adherents, and as many of them still remained with the British or lurked in secret places. And whereas, the commandant of Charleston, having sent beyond sea the wives and families of all the avowed friends of America in town and country; and the brigadiers of militia had been ordered to retaliate by sending the wives and families of such adherents within the British lines; and it is understood that they are in great distress and poverty. Therefore, a free pardon is offered for the offence of having borne arms, provided they surrender themselves up to a brigadier of the state within thirty days, and do constant duty in the militia service for six months; and upon performance of these conditions their wives and children were allowed to return; except such as having joined the enemy, were called upon by two proclamations to return in forty days, in pursuance of an ordinance of the legislature. All such as were sent out of the state for refusing to take the oath required of them by law and had returned. All such as subscribed addresses to Sir H. Clinton and Lord Cornwallis, congratulating them on their victories. All such as hold or have held military commissions. And all those whose conduct has been so infamous that they cannot consistent with policy and justice partake of the rights of citizens. But if they surrender to the commander in chief for the time, and were judged inadmissible, they should not be detained."

This abstract has been given to show the singular manner of legislating in those times.[27] Not, but that it was necessary thus to legislate, as it was certainly better to have some kind of civil government than none. The raising of two regiments of cavalry was suggested by Gen. Greene, and highly approved both by the governor and Marion, and it certainly promised well at first. Col. Hezekiah Maham, who had been elected by the provincial congress a captain in the first rifle regiment, when they passed an act to raise two such regiments, in March, 1776, was now appointed commander of one corps, and Col. Peter Horry commander of the other; he had been captain in the 2d regiment from the beginning of 1775, and was the older officer of the two; the reader will hereafter see the effect of this observation.

As they had no bounty money to give, recruiting went on slowly, and they fell upon the following expedient, which was warmly opposed by Gov. Rutledge at first, but it is supposed was favoured by Marion. All men that could hire a substitute in the regiments now raising were exempted from militia duty.—This soon drew from the ranks the best of Marion's men, men who had served from the first, and had left their families at home in huts, and still in distress; but they could yet spare one or two negroes, which they did not much value, to hire a substitute to do duty for them. The war was now moved

Chapter 3: Campaign of 1781

comparatively far from them, and they sighed for home. In the mean time, the six months men came tumbling in by scores, to supply their places. Their new white feathers, fine coats, new saddles and bridles, and famished horses, showed they had lately been in the British garrison. These were not the men to endure privations and fight their country's battles. Those of Marion's tried men who remained, could never confide in them; and now, as is always usual in armies, the most unprincipled men enlisted in the new regiments, but were not kept in the discipline necessary for taming such characters, or making them good soldiers. When Maham had got about seventy men and Horry not yet a troop, both their commissions being of the same date, they quarreled about precedence in rank; and although Gov. Rutledge reasoned, Gen. Greene persuaded, and Marion threatened, they could never be reconciled. Maham appears to have been very refractory on this occasion, and would listen to no accommodation. While in the end, Horry acted much in the wrong.

There are in the correspondence of that day many letters of Gov. Rutledge, several of which, without the suppression of names, it would be highly injurious to the feelings of many to publish at the present time; the rest are not interesting, except a few which show the spirit of the times; and are mostly long and able constructions of militia laws, now obsolete. About this time he issued a proclamation suspending the acts of assembly, and making paper money[28] a tender in law, which, although strong, was certainly a just proceeding.

Col. Maham having now raised and equipped part of his cavalry, passed the Santee, burnt some British stores in the house of Sir John Colleton, at Fairlawn, and took some prisoners. On the 16th of October, Gen. Greene writes to Marion, "Col. Maham's success is highly honourable to himself and corps, and I hope will be followed by future strokes of good fortune." This hope was not realized. A letter from Col. Doyle, of the British, shows strongly what different views, men engaged on opposite sides, will take of the same transaction. It is to Gen. Marion: "Sir, I am directed by Brigadier Gen. Stewart, to represent to you an outrage that has been committed by a party of your corps, under the command of Col. Maham, upon a parcel of sick, helpless soldiers in an hospital at Colleton house, on the morning of the 17th inst. The burning an hospital, and dragging away a number of dying people to expire in swamps, is a species of barbarity hitherto unknown in civilized warfare. The general expects that those unhappy sufferers will be sent immediately as prisoners upon parole. Attacks on hospitals are, among your own continental army, unprecedented. The hospital at Camden was by Gen. Greene's order protected, although it had an armed guard for its internal police." Gen. Greene, who ere this, the reader must have perceived, was polite to his friends, and humane to his enemies, for even they are obliged to confess it, immediately instituted an inquiry into this complaint;[29] but how it was accommodated cannot now be ascertained.

On the 9th October, 1781, Gen. Marion received the most agreeable news of the surrender of Lord Cornwallis, and the next evening gave a fete to the ladies of Santee, at the house of Mr. John Cantey. The general's heart was not very susceptible of the gentler emotions; he had his friend, and was kind to his inferiors, but his mind was principally absorbed by the love of country; and as the capture of Lord Cornwallis was intimately connected with this passion there is no doubt he felt joy on the occasion. But if he did feel joy upon a few occasions, certain it is that watchful anxiety was the daily inmate of his breast.

On the same day he received the thanks of congress "for his wise, decided and gallant conduct, in defending the liberties of his country, and particularly for his prudent and intrepid attack on a body of British troops on the 31st day of August last; and for the distinguished part he took in the battle of the 8th Sept." Immediately on receiving the intelligence of the capture of Lord Cornwallis, Gen. Greene prepared for moving his army into the lower country. On the 5th November, he writes to Gen. Marion, "Gen. Sumter has orders to take post at Orangeburgh, to prevent the tories in that quarter from conveying supplies to town, and his advanced parties will penetrate as low as Dorchester; therefore you may act in conjunction with him, or employ your troops on the enemy's left, as you may find from information, they can best be employed. Please to give me your opinion on which side they can be most useful." Gen. Marion four days after passed the Santee, and in a short time took post near Huger's bridge, as it was still termed, though all the bridges in the lower country were taken down, except the one at Goose creek, which seemed to be left by mutual consent of both armies, for the purpose of reaching one another, by at least one way. He arrived at Huger's bridge in the night, and in less than an hour after detached a strong party by the heads of Huger's and Quimby creeks, to Cainhoy, in St. Thomas'. On the 23d November Gen. Sumter was posted at Orangeburgh; on the 17th of the same month Gen. Greene marched for the Fourholes. December 7th, he lay at Jacksonborough, and on the 13th of the same month, he encamped at the Round O.

His movements were at this time cautious, in keeping both the Edisto and Ashley between himself and the enemy; because he had heard they were reinforced, and he was as yet without ammunition. He wrote now frequently to Gen. Marion, and almost every letter has a clause similar to the one of the 15th of November: "You are at liberty to act as you think advisable. I have no particular instructions to give you, and only wish you to avoid surprise."

At the close of this year, Gov. Rutledge and his council issued writs of election for members of the senate and house of representatives, which, by proclamation issued afterwards, were appointed to meet at Jacksonborough. Gen. Greene still lay at the Round O, where he secured the rice and other provisions from the enemy, by sending out patroles of cavalry as far as Dorchester: but he had not yet received a supply of ammunition for his infantry, and Marion was also without that indispensible muniment of war. As to other necessaries he says, "Our horsemen have neither cloaks or blankets, nor have our troops received a shilling of pay since they came into this country. Nor is there a prospect of any. Yet they do not complain."[30] At length on the 14th of December he received a supply of ammunition and sent it all to Marion, then at Watboo, saying, "he was in expectation of soon receiving more."

The British extended their patroles of cavalry nearly up to Dorchester, but their main body was now confined to Charleston neck.

Thus, in the course of the campaign of 1781, the American army under Gen. Greene, without pay, without clothing, and as we have seen frequently without ammunition, had driven the enemy from all their strong holds but one; had defeated them in battle, and retaken all South Carolina but a neck of land.

* * * * *

Detached Narratives for 1781

There was with Marion's brigade throughout, a young man, Robert, commonly called Bob James, but oftener, the general's right hand man. It was known to very few that Marion employed him often to gain intelligence from the enemy in Georgetown and other places. The general never suffered him to mount guard or do common duties; being an excellent woodsman, he was his favourite guide; being an expert swimmer, he was generally by his side when swimming rivers, or paddled him over in a canoe if they had one; being a good fisherman, he often caught him fish; the general would laugh and joke with him, but with no other private. He did not however employ Bob in these small matters when he had any thing serious for him to do. Surprised at his exact intelligence from Georgetown and other places, the author asked him once "how he got it?" He related several interesting particulars, among others this one: "Just in the outskirts of Georgetown there is a pond full of bushes, and in the middle of it a large gum-tree with a thick top and branches that reach the thicket below. This tree overlooked the garrison and both roads leading out of town. I used to climb into it and watch for days together, and if I saw any thing important, immediately came down, mounted my horse, hid in a neighbouring swamp, and told it to the general myself, or sent the only other person we trusted." The gum tree stood there lately, but Robert James sleeps with his fathers. "Alas, poor Yorick! I knew him Horatio." It was generally thought that although he swam so often on horseback, or crossed rivers in unsteady canoes, the general could not swim himself. His body was sufficient for endurance; and his mind, to sagacity and foresight, united the higher virtues of patience and fortitude. In one thing he appeared singular; long swords were now in fashion as best for attack or defence, but Gen. Marion always wore the little cut and thrust, which was in use in the second regiment, and he was seldom, perhaps never, seen to draw it. His messmates told a story, whether true or not is of little consequence, as it shows the public opinion. The sum of this story was, that on one occasion he attempted to draw it, but it was so rusty he could not extricate it from the scabbard. He had a reason for this apparent singularity; a long sword might have tempted him, a small man, to act the common soldier, and he appeared to place no reliance on his personal prowess. Gen. Greene depended entirely upon him for intelligence.—Now, intelligence is the life of an army. Sumter and Greene were then at variance, and if Sumter gained any, he would not condescend to let Greene know it, but take advantage of it himself. Lee, whose particular business it was to furnish Greene with intelligence, was always too fond of seeing his men and horses in good plight, to expose them to hardships. Marion's were for every day's use.

An anecdote worthy to be recorded happened at the brick house at the Eutaw. Capt. Laurence Manning, since adjutant general in this state, marched at the head of the legion infantry to batter down the door of the house. Intent on this single object, and relying confidently on his men, he advanced boldly up to the door; when, looking behind him for the first time, behold his men had deserted him. He stood for a moment at the side of the door, revolving what was to be done.—Fortunately a British officer, Capt. Barry, opened the door gently to peep out, and Manning seizing him fast by the collar, jerked him out. He then used him as an ancient warrior would have done his shield, and the enemy, fearing to shoot least they should kill Barry, Manning escaped without a shot being fired at him from the house.

During the struggle of the present year, (1781) Capt. Wm. Allston, of True Blue, on Little river, All Saints parish, served under Gen. Marion. He was a firm patriot and good soldier; indeed he may well be enumerated among the martyrs to the cause of his country; for having been seized with a fever in camp, he had scarcely time to reach his home, where he expired at a middle age. He left behind him, by his last wife, two sons and a daughter; his eldest son he named after the illustrious Washington; and he has since proved himself to be highly worthy of that distinction. In this son will be readily recognised the distinguished artist, Washington Allston; whose pencil has bestowed celebrity upon the place of his birth, and whom every American should be proud to claim as his countryman.

Towards the conclusion of this year, Maj. Edward Hyrne, one of Gen. Greene's aids, was commissioned by him to negociate a cartel of exchange of prisoners in Charleston. He had to conduct this with Col. Balfour, who was haughty and unreasonable as well as cruel; his demands were so exorbitant, that Maj. Hyrne, after waiting upon him several times with much patience, at length declared they were utterly inadmissible, and took his leave. Returning

Chapter 3: Campaign of 1781

to his lodgings, he wrote a note to each British officer on parole in town, informing him he must prepare to follow him into the country the next day. His firmness or good policy had the desired effect; Balfour's quarters were soon besieged by at least forty officers, many of whom were of higher rank than himself, and Major Hyrne succeeded to the extent of his wishes.

The party under Major John Postell, which was ordered out on the 29th January in this year, and succeeded in taking eleven British waggons with soldiers' clothing at Keithfield, consisted with the officers, commanding of thirty-eight men. They carried off what clothing they could, and what they could not they burnt. What was carried away was sold for a division, and bought in, as it appears, in continental dollars, on the 2d February, 1781.

The prices of a few are inserted; sixteen blankets were sold.

1 Bought by Major Postell for	$1590
1 do. Capt. Wm. Capers	2200
1 do. (the lowest priced) by Capt. Thomas Potts,	900
1 Loaf of sugar, Francis Greene,	2000
1 Coat by Capt. Capers,	6210
1 Knife and fork, A. Simons,	700
1 Pair of Stockings, Capt. Capers,	800

Most of this party were supernumerary officers, who placed themselves under the command of Major (then Captain) Postell, who was justly considered as one of the most enterprising officers in Marion's brigade. Of these thirty-eight men, the only survivor is Richard Greene, who has been long a respectable and opulent planter on Black river. The account of sales is in the hand writing of Capt. Thomas Potts. There is a list of the names of the thirty-eight, many of whom fought then and afterwards with great bravery.—John Futhey, then a lieutenant, after being promoted to a captaincy was killed in a skirmish at Avant's ferry on Black river. Thomas Potts, jun. a lieutenant, was twice wounded. John M'Bride, father of the late friend of the author, Dr. James M'Bride, was always at his post. What a loss to science was the early death of the son? Capt. Wm. Capers was imprisoned by Balfour in the upper story of his provost, and made his escape by slipping past the keeper at night when he brought their scanty supper to the prisoners. He had then to descend a steep flight of stairs and pass the guard at the bottom. Luckily he stumbled at the head of the stairs and fell to the bottom, and the guard mistaking him for the keeper, raised him up and gave him much consolation. He had only to refrain from speaking and to utter a few groans, which being an indistinct tone of the voice, made no discovery, and the guard suffered him to pass. A friend furnished him with a small boat to pass Cooper river; but now the difficulty was to get through the British guard ships which lined the river. Being a pretty good mimic, he bethought himself of assuming the character of a drunken sailor going on board his own ship, and acted his part so admirably well, that he was suffered, though often threatened, to pass through the whole fleet. Capt. Capers lost no time in joining Gen. Marion, with whom he fought bravely in the ranks until the general advanced down into St. Thomas' parish, where he commanded a company, and where he had left property at the mercy of the enemy.[31] Capt. Wm. Capers, and his brother G. Sinkler Capers, were often afterwards the terror of the enemy, who had early oppressed and imprisoned them, for G. S. Capers had also made his escape from the provost.

Francis G. Deliesseline, the present sheriff of Charleston district, joined Marion when a boy, and made if possible a still more surprising and narrow escape out of the same provost; but as the narrative would expose certain names which he wishes concealed, he has declined giving it publicity. At so early an age, none behaved better than Deliesseline, and no one has refreshed the author's memory more in the detail of facts of that period.

Many of the privates of Marion's brigade were men of character and honour; most of them lost their fortunes by the war, and many made them, or at least handsome competencies, after it; but it is believed that more, cast out of the ways of industry and economy, and losing their all, sunk under the pressure brought upon them. Where they are known, what an injustice would it be to pass over the merits of such men?—On the monument erected by the Greeks at Thermopylae, the names of Leonidas and his three hundred men were not inscribed, because it was thought impossible to imagine they could ever be forgotten.

Pardon me, ye sons of my fellow soldiers! should my memory be found not so tenacious; and should I have passed over the merits of many of your fathers without even a shade of remembrance.

Footnotes

1. This was the same Rugely who behaved so generously to Governor Rutledge. It seems Lord Cornwallis intended to have promoted him, but after this affair he wrote to Tarleton, "Rugely will not be made a brigadier."
2. Marion's letter, 22d February.
3. Letter of Marion, 7th March.
4. About ten days, as it appears from the dates of his letters.
5. This young lady was Mary, the second daughter of John Witherspoon, who after the war, was married to Conyers. One day when her lover made his appearance as usual, a British officer made use of language disrespectful to him, which she bore for some time with patience; at last he said something indelicate to herself. She im-

Chapter 3: Campaign of 1781

mediately drew off a walking shoe from her foot, and flung it in his face, saying, "coward! go meet him." In those days kid slippers were not fashionable.

6. Horry's Narrative.

7. Greene's letters, 4th and 17th April.

8. Gen. Greene's elegant letter to Marion, 9th May.

9. Marion's letter, 23d April.

10. By a copy of Major Postell's parole, preserved in Horry's correspondence, it appears he was paroled in Charleston; but, soon after, the British or tories stripped him of all his property, which was a breach of it on their part. In a letter to Gen. Marion, 14th Jan. he says, "My honour is all I have left—my family has been reduced to beg their bread."

11. This is partly extracted from Lee's Memoirs.

12. Capt. Smith, afterwards well known in this state as Col. John Smith, of Darlington, surrendered himself prisoner to a lieutenant of the British; and after he had delivered his sword, was struck by the lieutenant with the broad side of it. At the battle of Guilford, Smith had killed Col. Stewart, of the British guards, in a single rencounter; and his bravery was otherwise so well known that the British officers invited him to a dinner in Camden. Before dinner, he mentioned how he had been treated by the lieutenant, and it was agreed among them, that, as that officer was to be present at the dinner, Smith should be at liberty to treat him as he thought fit. Accordingly Smith kicked him down stairs; and as he did not resent it, he was soon after cashiered.

13. As all the accounts of the movements of Greene and Col. Lee, into South Carolina, are confused, from a want of information of the local situation of the country, and the clashing of the names of places; the present note has been subjoined to rectify misconceptions. From Ensign Johnson Baker's account we have seen Lee at the Long bluff, since called Greenville, now Society-hill. At that time, the marshes of Black creek, and the bogs of Black river, were impassable (except to Marion,) on any direct route to Camden, or Scott's lake, or Santee; but there was an Indian path, by the way of the present Darlington court house and Day's ferry, on Lynch's creek, to Kingstree; and from the latter place there was a road to Murray's ferry on Santee. From the necessity of the case, therefore, this must have been Lee's route, for he cannot explain it himself. Lee had been the principal adviser of Greene to return to South Carolina, for which the country can never be too grateful to him; and being now about to invest fort Watson, he sent Dr. Matthew Irvine, for whom both leaders had a great friendship, and who, from his persuasive powers was highly fitted for the mission, to inspire Greene with hope and confidence. Irvine obtained a guide and an escort from Col. Richardson, and proceeded by the route of the Piny lands, back of the Santee hills, then a pathless wilderness, now a thickly settled country, and on the first broad road he fell in with in this tract, he unexpectedly met with Greene, about fifteen miles from Camden. Irvine continued with him, until descending a range of Sand hills between little and great Pinetree creeks, about a mile from Camden, he crossed great Pinetree creek at the place now called M'Crae's mill. From the latter place, Greene proceeded about three miles to an old mill on Town creek, called English's; and here Irvine left him, and Cantey met with him as a general and his army emerging from the wilderness. This first broad road must again from the necessity of the case, for there was no other at that time, have been the road from Cheraw hill to Camden. Thus have the

accounts of two respectable witnesses, Dr. Irvine and Gen. Cantey, been reconciled, which appeared at first sight impossible.

14. Major Burnet's letter, 28th April. He was aid to Gen. Greene.

15. Nothing shows the moderation of Gen. Marion more than this simple matter of fact. Although the country at that time was plundered and miserably poor, yet he had only to express a wish and he would have had a dozen homespun blankets. He had then in his pocket a power from the governor to impress them.

16. Dr. Irvine was riding between Cols. Lee and Maham, and was wounded by a discharge of small arms from the enemy, as they wheeled at a short turn of the road. Lee had two surgeons in his corps, Irvine and Skinner; Irvine was apt to expose himself to danger, but Skinner, although he had on one occasion killed his adversary in a duel, was a coward; and the method he now took to punish Irvine for what he called his temerity, was not to dress his wounds until the last.

17. Lee states that he found such a chasm in the bridge his men could not cross it.

18. These St. Augustine friends, were sixty-two influential characters, citizens of Charleston, whom Lord Cornwallis, soon after the town surrendered, had ordered to be sent and imprisoned at St. Augustine, contrary to the terms of the capitulation.

19. Vatt. B.1.C.13. S.170-2. Montesq. B.6.C.3.

20. It is believed, at English's ferry, nine miles below Camden.

21. Col. Doyle gives him that title in a letter hereafter noticed.

22. Plenty of water might have been procured, in Eutaw creek, some hundred yards from the battle ground; and why the retreat was not directed there, or to Santee river, distant a mile, the author is at a loss to discover: unless it was that Greene's force was scattered up the road, and he wished to concentrate it. It was not from dread of the enemy.

23. Maj. Marjoribanks, by whom in conjunction with Sheridan, the British army was saved, lies buried on the Santee canal road, about half a mile below the chapel; he was a brave and generous enemy; and on an old head board, the following inscription is still to be seen: "JOHN MARJORIBANKS, Esqr. late major to the 19th regt. inf'y and commanding a flank bat'n. of his majesty's army. Obiit. 22d October, 1781."

24. Very soon after the revolutionary war, this scene was entirely changed. Planters, in clearing their land, had rolled logs and other rubbish from their fields, into the lakes and creeks leading from the river, and many threw trees into it to get them quickly out of the way. The upper country also soon became more opened, and gave freer vent from above to the waters. There came on a succession of six or seven years, which were wet; and the consequence was, that the usual passages for the waters below being obstructed, they flooded the low grounds, and ruined the planters. Where fine corn grew at that time, trees may now be seen a foot and a half in diameter, in the midst of briars and cane brakes.

25. Commonly called mutton corn, a corruption of matin, that is early corn.

26. Instance—New England rum at $3 75. Soldier's saddles $25. Blankets none as yet. Best indigo in exchange three shillings sterling. Letter 9th October.

27. Governor Rutledge had but two of his council with him at this time, Daniel Huger and John L. Gervais.

28. For an example of its present depreciation, see p. 152. [Detached Narratives for 1781, Paragraph 6—list of prices.—A. L.]

29. Greene's letter, 24th Nov.
30. Greene's letters, 13th and 14th December.
31. The following is a curious fact in natural history. When Capt. G. S. Capers returned to his plantation in 1782, it had been completely stripped of all live stock and poultry, except one cock. When the British chased him he had always taken refuge under a kitchen low to the ground. This bird was carefully preserved. After the war, it was the fashion for ladies to wear scarlet cloaks, and so strong was his recollection (must it be so called) of the colour of the British uniform, that whenever he saw ladies in scarlet cloaks, he would squall out, as such birds usually do at sight of danger, and run directly under the kitchen.

Chapter 4:

Campaign of 1782

The military history of this year, is not remarkable for any great events; but the most material of these happened in the brigade of Marion. As they are not altogether of a pleasant nature, it appears to have been the wish of many to bury them in oblivion, and therefore some of them have been suppressed, and others but slightly recorded. But, the correspondence gives dates and hints, which bring the whole to recollection; and it is the duty of the biographer to be impartial. It was hoped that he might have avoided saying any thing more about the dispute which arose between Cols. Peter Horry and Maham; but, as that dispute terminated in unhappy consequences, it becomes necessary that they should be developed. Gen. Marion was returned, at the elections which took place for the Jacksonborough assembly, a member of the senate for St. John's, Berkley. Being about to take his seat, he gave the immediate command of the brigade to Col. Peter Horry,[1] subject to his future order. Of this order, all that is necessary to state here, is as follows: "You will take command of my brigade until I return. You will keep the guards at Cainhoy and Fogartie's. Their orders are to prevent any boats or persons from going to or from town, without a written pass from me or yourself. Col. Maham's corps will be ordered to Mepkin, to remain there until my further orders." As the enemy got most of their intelligence from persons, more especially women, going to and from town, this part of the order was very material. In the mean time application was made by Gen. Marion to Greene to decide this unhappy dispute between the colonels; and, in a conciliating letter, he decided it in favour of Horry. (16th Jan.) On the 18th of January, Gen. Marion writes to Horry: "I send you Gen. Greene's letter in answer to mine, sent him as soon as I arrived here, and it is determined as I expected. You will keep the letter, and if the enemy should approach your quarters, and you find it necessary, you must call on Col. Maham's troops and horse, as reinforcements; and I wish he may not be called upon for any other purpose." In a letter from Col. Maham to Horry, of the 20th of January, it is to be inferred that the latter had immediately called upon him for a return of his corps, and to submit to his orders; for he answers, "I cannot think of being commanded by an officer of the same rank. I think it proper not to make you any return of my regiment, and I shall not obey any order you may be pleased to send." It appears from a subsequent letter of Maham's of the same date, that Gen. Marion had not

Chapter 4: Campaign of 1782

written to him concerning the determination of Gen. Greene; but Gen. Marion's order, both then and subsequently, was certainly sufficient to convince him he ought to submit. After this Col. Horry writes to Gen. Marion: "Col. Maham interferes with my command so much that I can scarcely act; he gave passes to several ladies to go to town without my leave, and they accordingly went in a boat, which boat has since returned, and the ladies have since come up." And again, "I assure you your presence is much wanted. Your brigade lessens daily." (31st Jan.) On the 3d of February, Marion answers: "I am surprised at Col. Maham's interference with your command. I have written him positive orders not to do so in any respect whatever, and was in hopes Gen. Greene would have prevented such evils before this." But from a former letter of Gov. Rutledge, which is a philippic against Horry, and the subsequent determination of Gov. Matthews, it is evident that Maham had got the civil authority on his side, and he did not regard the general's. And thus it is, when civilians interfere with military affairs that they invariably commit blunders. Having premised these facts, to show that in Marion's absence there was naught but discord and dissention, we now proceed to state the consequences.

Almost the whole of the warfare was henceforth carried on in St. Thomas' and St. James', Santee. About this time, Col. Richard Richardson commanded the post at Cainhoy. A British galley lay in the river Wando, which he watched, and patroled the road down to Daniel's island by day, and returned into the woods and lay without fire by night. A fortnight after he was posted there, hearing of a party of British which had landed at Daniel's island, he immediately sent out scouts to the causeway over to the island, and wrote for a reinforcement. In the morning Maham's horse arrived, four troops in uniform, and fully equipt; but their colonel, who would have been ranked by Richardson, was not present, and they were under the command of Maj. Giles. The British took the Strawberry road, and about noon stopped at Bishop Smith's, Brabant, about fourteen miles up the road. To the north of that plantation is a swamp of considerable width, with a causeway and bridge. Beyond the causeway, on the right going up, was a fence on a bank and a ditch behind it, with trees in front. Richardson passed the swamp above, and going down to the hill above this fence, immediately went to reconnoitre, but came back with a British troop and Capt. Campbell at his heels. He ordered a charge. At the commencement of the onset it was easy to be seen that Maham's corps had not yet been trained. They charged in some disorder, but at first drove the British horse easily before them. At the bridge they met the British infantry, who gave them a volley. All was now confusion, horses and men wedged together upon a narrow causeway. The front striving to retreat, and the rear urging them on. The British horse being rallied, now came in to aid the infantry, and a total rout and scene of carnage ensued. Of Maham's officers, Capt. Samuel Cooper rallied his men, and returning to the road, saved several lives and drove back a troop of black dragoons. In this affair the six months men particularly suffered. Being near the road when the rout commenced, they wheeled their lean horses and ran directly up it, consequently they were trampled down by both parties. Capt. Bennett, with twelve men, after having been pursued by a party of British, double his number, and stopped by an impassable creek, when inspiring his men with courage, and setting the example, they wheeled about and drove back the enemy. In the course of this day, G. S. Capers took three swords from the British in single rencounters, and Gen. Marion promoted him to a lieutenancy. It appears that the defeat might have been prevented if Richardson had posted his militia behind the fence described. Twenty-two Americans were buried on the causeway; how many were killed in the pursuit is not known. Of the British, Capt. Campbell was killed, and several of his men, but the number was not ascertained.

Gen. Marion had now taken his seat in the senate at Jacksonborough; but his presence, as will shortly be seen, was much more necessary in camp; but he could not get leave of absence, nor be spared without breaking up the house, for there were but thirteen senators present, which number was required as a quorum to do business. They were passing a new militia act, and one for raising the continental quota of troops for the state; and the confiscation act at that time and place was esteemed of greater consequence than the commanding of a brigade. But in all his letters dated from that place, Gen. Marion expresses the utmost anxiety to return to his command.

In the mean time Horry, by orders of Gen. Marion, took a position on the north side of Wambaw, a large creek emptying into the Santee. He lay in the angle formed by the two roads which pass from Lenud's ferry road to Mr. Horry's, about a quarter of a mile from the bridge. In his rear there was a wood. His new raised regiment, scarcely yet half completed, lay at Durant's plantation about a mile above, under the immediate command of Maj. Benson. On the 23d of February, Horry had out patroles upon the Christ Church road, and scouts down in St. Thomas'. Thinking himself secure, and being sick, on the 24th he went over the river to his plantation, and left the brigade under the command of Col. M'Donald, contrary to Gen. Marion's order, which was to leave it in such case under Maham. While Benson was at dinner, Capt. Bennett, who commanded the scouts in St. Thomas', came in with intelligence that the British were approaching, but at that time of day he was an unwelcome messenger. Bennett proceeded down to head quarters at Mr. Horry's, where M'Donald was also at dinner. He likewise would not believe the intelligence, because he said he had been down into Christ Church the day before; but he desired Maj. James who had just arrived in camp, and came for orders, to take command of his regiment. In less than half an hour after a firing commenced at Durant's. M'Donald's regiment was on the right towards Echaw, and two regiments of six months men on the left towards Wambaw. Maj. James im-

Chapter 4: Campaign of 1782

mediately formed M'Donald's regiment in the wood in the rear, and rode to the left for orders from the commanding officer present, Col. Screven; but when he arrived, Screven's men had broke, and he was in the act of rallying them, but the attempt was vain. They ran over the bridge and threw off the planks. Maj. James returned to his own men, and as fugitives were now passing in numbers from Horry's corps, he ordered a retreat to the bridge. As he brought up the rear and was on horseback, two British dragoons attempted in succession to cut him down, but he kept them in check with his pistols, and finally leaped a chasm in the bridge, supposed to be twenty feet in width. He by this means gained time to rally his men, and checked the British.

Thus Gen. Marion had not left his brigade more than six weeks, before it had dwindled away and had been defeated. On the part of Horry's cavalry it was a complete surprise. Major Benson was killed, and what number of men cannot be ascertained, but he lost thirty-five horses.

The British were commanded by Col. Thompson, afterwards the celebrated Count Rumford. Maham having refused to cooperate with Horry, lay still at Mepkin; and Gen. Marion passing there on the 24th, took command of his corps and proceeded towards Wambaw; but the colonel was not present. On his way Gen. Marion was sorely vexed with the disagreeable news of the defeat of his brigade; but with such a fine corps as Maham's was then he felt sure of beating the enemy should they appear. He proceeded down to Mrs. Tiddiman's plantation, between Echaw and Wambaw, and there halted for provisions. (25th Feb.) There was a lane with a high fence on each side, leading up to the house, and the cavalry picketted in the lane. In front of the lane was an old field, and a little to the right a pond of water. Scarce half an hour had elapsed when the British appearing in the old field, displayed their columns and seemed to pause. Capt. John Carraway Smith commanded Maham's corps; he drew up his men in solid column, and Gen. Marion having posted a small body of infantry to great advantage along the fence of the lane, ordered Smith to charge. He proceeded very well till he got to the edge of the pond, where an inclination to the left was necessary to reach the enemy, but in performing this evolution his men fell into disorder, and the enemy charged with a shout. All was now rout and dismay; but the British followed no further than the edge of the woods. Gen. Marion had rallied a troop there, and checked the pursuit. The loss was but little; Lieut. Smizer and three men only were killed; but the disgrace was great. Had this corps been well trained the enemy must have been beaten. Horry had thus lost a great part of his horses, and Maham's corps was a second time shamefully defeated.

We have seen Count Rumford opposed to Gen. Marion with a degree of success, which perhaps he would not have obtained had the orders of the general been obeyed. It is well known that Count Rumford was a native of Massachusetts, and of the town there whence he took his title; also that he became after this a celebrated philosopher, and especially in economics; his writings have been of great use to the world. It is a pity that the career of such a man should have commenced in hostility to his native country. His life has been published, but we have not yet had the pleasure of reading it; and perhaps it may not contain the following anecdote. After his dashing success at the Santee he formed a grand scheme, which was no less than that of surprising Gen. Greene in his camp at Ashley hill. To effect this he must either have crossed Ashley river over Bacon bridge, at Dorchester, which was too well secured for a sudden attack of cavalry; or he must cross the river at Ashley ferry, ten miles from town. He determined on the latter, and put his four troops of cavalry in motion. When he arrived at the ferry it was ebb of tide, the water was running out as from a millsluice; the banks on each side were so miry as scarcely to support a crab—the river was at least one hundred yards wide, and there was not a boat.—He however ordered Major Fraser to lead on the first troop into the river and swim across. Fraser viewed him for some time with astonishment, suspecting him not to be in his sober senses. But finding he appeared so, he said to him, "Why, Sir, I am not in the habit of disputing, or hesitating to perform any order given by my commander; but this thing is utterly impossible." "How so," said Thompson, "it may be difficult but not impossible, and if we do not attempt difficult things we shall never be distinguished. Alexander swam across the Granicus, beat the Persians and immortalized himself." "And it would no doubt immortalize you," replied Fraser, "if you could swim the Ashley, and surprise Gen. Greene; but let us put the matter to the test. Here is Serjt. Allen, the best trooper and the best swimmer in the corps; and here is my horse that cost me one hundred guineas. Let Allen try it first; better that he than that all should be lost." The proposition was agreed to. Allen was mounted on the major's charger, and was ordered to swim the river.—"I'll try," said he, "since the colonel orders it—but the Lord have mercy upon me;" and having so said, he plunged into the river. As might have been expected, the current swept him a quarter of a mile below the landing on the opposite side; he attempted to land there, but the fine horse was swallowed up in the marsh, and Allen escaped with the utmost difficulty.—This was the last notice we have of Col. Thompson (Count Rumford) in this country: he was a burning meteor but soon disappeared.[2]

After the defeat at Wambaw, Gov. Matthews, having taken much pains to find out from Gen. Marion who was the best cavalry officer of the two, Horry or Maham, incorporated the two regiments and gave the command to the latter. The preference appears to have been extorted from Marion. The fact was that Horry, though said to be a good infantry officer, failed in one most essential requisite in the command of cavalry, and that was horsemanship. In several charges he made, it is said he was indebted to some one or other of his men for saving his life; yet possessing great personal bravery, his supreme delight was

Chapter 4: Campaign of 1782

always to be at the head of cavalry. From the commencement of this narrative, his patriotism has been conspicuous: in fact, his property was wasted and his life often exposed in the cause of his country, and few men were more devoted to her than Col. Peter Horry. He now resigned, but as some consolation, Gen. Marion made him commandant of Georgetown, with full powers to regulate its trade and defend it from the enemy. It was from thence and Cainhoy, that Gen. Marion after long perseverance, got much clothing for Greene's army. But Col. P. Horry, instead of leaving trade to flow into Georgetown as freely as the tides which passed before him, put it under such restrictions that the merchants soon began to murmur. About the 20th of April, there was an alarm excited among the civil authority of the state, that the British in Charleston had been reinforced and were about to attack Gen. Greene. Gov. Matthews immediately wrote to order Gen. Marion to his assistance. He lay at that time near Murray's ferry; his men had been dismounted by an order from the same authority, and they now set out for Bacon's bridge on foot for the first time. When they reached within eight miles, the alarm had subsided; but another had taken place, that the enemy had sailed for Georgetown, and the governor ordered Marion there. After a forced march of four days he arrived at White's bridge; but there was no enemy near Georgetown. In this march of about one hundred and sixty miles, Marion's men had but one ration of rice; all the rest were of lean beef driven out of the woods in the month of April. As Ganey's party had been troublesome to the people of North Carolina, and had not observed the treaty of neutrality with Gen. Marion, made June 17th, 1781, a joint expedition was concerted between Gov. Matthews, of South and Gov. Martin of North Carolina, to subdue them.[3] Of this expedition Gen. Marion was to have the command. His very name was sufficient for the purpose intended. At Burch's mill on Pedee, a treaty was signed, (June 1782) by which Ganey's party agreed to lay down their arms as enemies of the state, to demean themselves hereafter as peaceable citizens, to deliver up all stolen property, to apprehend all who did not accede to the treaty now made, to take all deserters from the American army and deliver them up, to return to their allegiance and abjure that of his Britannic majesty. From this treaty, Gibson, who killed Col. Kolb, and Fanning and his party were excepted, but they escaped. Fanning was properly of North Carolina, but occasionally acted with Ganey, and was one of the most active men, and one of the most deliberate murderers of the whole party. But little defence had been made by the tories; only one skirmish took place, in which the general's friend, Robert James, was wounded; and at the Bowling Green, between Great and Little Pedee, at least five hundred men laid down their arms to Gen. Marion. Thus ended an opposition to the country, which commenced more from the desire of plunder than from principle, and which, except with regard to sex, and some to age, had been carried on in the true spirit of savage warfare. Of Harrison's party, many had gone with him to the British; with those who remained a species of warfare was waged even after the peace with Great Britain.

During Gen. Marion's absence, Gen. Greene appears, from the correspondence, to have been very anxious for his return. After the adjournment of the Jacksonborough assembly, he had crossed the Edisto and encamped on the west side of Ashley river, sixteen miles from Charleston, and here the sufferings of his men had risen to the utmost extremity. They were often without rations, and when served, it was generally with lean meat without bread or rice, or bread or rice without the lean meat. They had as yet received no pay, and their clothes were so worn and broken, that they were as naked as the Caffres of Africa. Here, in a state of inaction, they became mutinous, and were plotting to deliver up their commander to the enemy. But it is surprising, that when mischief of any kind began to brew in such a situation, that only twelve should have been concerned in it, and it is honourable that none of those were native Americans.

About the 9th of July, Gen. Marion had returned to the Santee, and received orders from Gen. Greene to remain between that and Cooper river, as heretofore. The militia were now so far relieved, that, by law, they were obliged to turn out only one month in three; but were ordered, as we have mentioned above, to be dismounted, which discouraged them, and rendered their movements less rapid. The experience derived both from the history of the revolutionary and the late war, fully shows that the militia are effective only when mounted.

On the 25th of August, in this year, Lieut. Col. John Laurens was killed in a skirmish at Page's point, on Combahee river. He fell in the flower of his youth, and yet had long been the admiration of both the contending armies. In history the parallel to his character is perhaps to be found only in that of the Chevalier Bayard: the knight without fear and without reproach.

During the remainder of the summer of 1782, Gen. Marion frequently changed his encampments from place to place, between Cooper and Santee rivers, with three objects constantly in view; to cut off supplies from the enemy, to prevent all surprises from their sudden irruptions, and to provide for his own men.—His scouting parties still penetrated into St. Thomas' parish as far as Daniel's island and Clement's ferry. At the head of one of these Capt. G. S. Capers performed a gallant action. Having the command of only twelve men, he encountered a party of twenty-six of the British black dragoons, and cut them to pieces. They had at the time two or three of his neighbours in handcuffs as prisoners.

About the 25th of August in that year, Marion lay for some time at the plantation of Sir John Colleton, the first above Watboo bridge, on the south side of that creek. This with him appeared to be a favourite place of encampment. It had been deserted by the owner, who was attached to the enemy, and the mansion and two extensive ranges of negro and other outhouses were left open for

Chapter 4: Campaign of 1782

himself and men. He occupied the mansion and his men the outhouses, on the west towards the bridge; on the back of the outhouses to the east, and directly in front of the dwelling, there stretched towards the road an extensive avenue of old cedar trees, the trimming of which had been neglected for some years; and their long boughs now descended nearly to the ground. While encamped in this situation, Gen. Marion heard of the approach of Major Fraser with the British cavalry, towards the Santee, in his rear. On this side there was nothing but an open old field for a mile. None but the officers now had horses, and he immediately ordered out a party of these, under Capt. Gavin Witherspoon, to reconnoitre the enemy. They had advanced but little way in the woods beyond the old field, when the reconnoitring party were met by Major Fraser at the head of his corps of cavalry, and were immediately charged. A long chase commenced, which was soon observed by Marion, and he drew up his men under the thick boughs of the cedar trees. As the chase advanced towards him it became more and more interesting.—When in full view, either Witherspoon's horse had failed him, or he fell purposely in the rear to bring up his party, and a British dragoon was detached to cut him down. He advanced until nearly within his sword's length, and was rising in his stirrups to make sure of his blow, but Witherspoon had eyed him well, and at the instant, Parthian like, he fired the contents of his gun into his breast. The good omen excited much animation, and the British, still advancing, attempted to charge upon the left, but were received on that side with a well directed fire, which caused them to break and fly in great disorder. Had Gen. Marion's cavalry been present they might now have been cut to pieces; but scarcity of forage had induced him to quarter them at the distance of six miles. The enemy rallied and manoeuvred about in the old field for an hour, making several different feints of charging, but never coming in reach of Marion's fire, whose men stood firm at their post. Capt. Gillies of the British, and nine men and five horses were killed. The number of wounded could not be accurately ascertained; but as the firing was only at the distance of thirty paces, and was made with the usual charge of heavy buckshot, the proportion of these must have been greater than that of the killed on the usual computation. (29th Aug.) On the next day, Gen. Marion called out Capt. Witherspoon in front of the brigade, and gave him thanks for his many public services, but more particularly for the deed of yesterday.

Here ended the warfare of Marion. Its close was as the last ray of the setting sun; in his progress through the day, at times shining brightly; at others clouded with darkness: but at eventide descending with cheerful brilliancy. Should the exploits performed, or the number of the enemy cut off, not equal the expectation of the reader, he is requested to recollect the lapse of time which has intervened, and how many circumstances must have escaped the memory of the writer, and particularly, that the loss of Col. Watson, with whom Marion had the most arduous of all his conflicts, could never be known. He will also bear in mind the patroles which went out nightly, and seldom failed to do some execution, which like a perpetual dripping corroded deeply into the force of the enemy. If the late Guerilla warfare in Spain cut off so many thousands of the French in detail, in a comparatively open country, how much more effect would such a warfare have in woods upon an enemy more weak in proportion and more slowly reinforced. Such a warfare is the one most fitted for militia and the most dreaded by regular troops. But on the other hand, should it be thought by some that the present narrative is too highly coloured, the eulogy of Gen. Greene, certainly the best judge of Gen. Marion's merit, is here inserted, of which it may be remarked, that it was written before the latter had performed half of what is here related.

Extract of a letter from Gen. Greene to Gen. Marion.

"Camp, before Camden, April 24, 1781.
Dear Sir,
Your favour of the 21st has just come to hand. When I consider how much you have done and suffered, and under what disadvantage you have maintained your ground, I am at a loss which to admire most, your courage and fortitude, or your address and management. Certain it is, no man has a better claim to the public thanks than you. History affords no instance wherein an officer has kept possession of a country under so many disadvantages as you have. Surrounded on every side with a superior force, hunted from every quarter with veteran troops; you have found means to elude their attempts and to keep alive the expiring hopes of an oppressed militia, when all succour seemed to be cut off. To fight the enemy bravely with the prospect of victory is nothing, but to fight with intrepidity under the constant impression of a defeat, and inspire irregular troops to do it, is a talent peculiar to yourself. Nothing will give me greater pleasure than to do justice to your merit, and I shall miss no opportunity of declaring to congress, the commander in chief of the American army, and to the world, the great sense I have of your merit and services."

The letters of Gen. Greene show that he was an agreeable polished gentleman. Their style is easy, simple and correct; there is no search after ornament; they come at once to the point and show him to be much in earnest. His commands are always requests, and when he might well have used the language of reprehension, it is only that of persuasion and friendly admonition. His privations here were great, perhaps he had not even the comforts of a common soldier in the British army; yet he states them fairly, without uttering a word of complaint; hopes they will soon be remedied, and declares his unalterable perseverance in gaining the glorious prize constantly in his view—the independence of his country.

Chapter 4: Campaign of 1782

In reviewing the transactions of the present year, two things passed which are well worth notice. Gen. Alexander Leslie, now commander in chief of the British army, a gentleman of enlarged views and humane feelings, had before this time, as it appears, submitted certain papers to Gen. Greene, through Capt. Skelly, for his inspection, preparatory to a proposal for a cessation of hostilities; and on the 23d of May, writes again to Greene in substance as follows: "Believing that a treaty for terminating the war is now carrying on, I have therefore to inform you, that those papers were transmitted to him (Gen. Leslie) by his excellency Sir Henry Clinton. That such was the manner in which those important papers had reached him, that he held it a duty he owed the rights of humanity, the welfare of this country, and the sentiments of the legislature of his own, to propose a cessation of hostilities." Again, on the 13th of August, Leslie proposed, "That the garrison of Charleston should be permitted to receive rice and other provisions, for which a compensation should be made on terms of mutual advantage." Both these propositions were at once rejected by the civil authority of the state; because it was supposed that Leslie only intended to amass provisions for the support of the British forces in the West Indies, to carry on war to advantage with our allies the French. But this matter might easily have been adjusted by treaty, and the rejection of the offer was certainly another piece of blind policy in the civil authority. They had now no means of taking the town, and by acceding to the proposals, Greene's army might have been clothed, the wants of the citizens sooner supplied, and much effusion of blood prevented.

Early in the month of January, in this year, the Jacksonborough assembly commenced its session. As might have been expected, it was entirely composed of those, who either in a civil or military capacity, had distinguished themselves in the late contest. In the senate we have seen there were but thirteen members, which was a bare quorum; and Gen. Marion could not be spared, for it would have broken up the house. In the house of representatives, there were but seventy-four members, of whom sixty formed a quorum. Both houses were therefore remarkably thin; but what they lacked in numbers they made up in spirit. They passed the well known confiscation law, avowedly to retaliate on the British for having acted in like manner to those who had adhered to the Americans; but privately with a view to enable the state to raise its quota of continental troops; for Gen. Marion, in a letter to Col. Peter Horry, of the 10th of February, states, that "Two regiments are to be raised, as our continental quota, giving each man a negro per year, which is to be taken from the confiscated estates. A number of large estates are down on this list, and others are amerced, which will give us at least a million sterling as a fund." And a clause in the act passed, enacts, "that there shall be set apart a sufficient number of slaves to raise the quota of continental troops required of this state." How far this law might be justified, on the plea of necessity and self-defence, is quite a different ground from that of retaliation. In the preamble to the law, the reason given for enacting it is retaliation upon tories for the injuries done to the property of the whigs by confiscations; but there appears to be no sound reason for passing the law as a retaliatory measure. Between rulers and subjects, or citizens, the duties of subjection and protection are reciprocal; but, in this case, the rulers were unable to protect the citizens, and therefore ought not to have expected from them such implicit subjection. It was only by a few daring spirits, and that generally in places remote from the enemy, that resistance was kept up; yet, under existing circumstances, it was not to be looked for from the timid more immediately in their power. But, as a measure of self-defence, the law was justifiable.

The governor and council, armed with the supreme power of the state, had impressed the horses, provisions and indigo of the whigs, for public services, and that proceeding had scarcely excited a murmur. These resources had now failed, and the war was to be carried on without money; then what good reason could be given for exempting from requisition the negroes and other property of the tories. In this point of view the case against them becomes the strongest of the two. Yet the clamour raised against the law at the time and after, was great; in the legislature their friends became numerous, and as each particular case was brought forward and considered, it was made an exception, and the act became a nullity. John Matthews was elected governor of the state, after Gen. Gadsden, for whom a majority of votes was first given, had declined serving. A bill was brought in to indemnify several militia officers who had been concerned in impressing indigo and other property necessary for public service. Gen. Marion's name was at first inserted on the list, but when it came to be read in the senate, he rose and moved to strike it out; saying, if he had taken the property of any man improperly or unnecessarily, he was willing to make restitution. The bill passed into a law without the general's name. Before the adjournment, the powers left with the governor and council, were as extensive as usual. Gov. Matthews appears to consider them in a letter to Gen. Leslie, (12th April) as equal to dispensing with parts of the confiscation act. The evacuation of Charleston took place on the 14th of December, 1782, but the militia were not permitted to be witnesses of the ceremony. The civil authority had interposed to exclude them as dangerous spectators, and Gen. Greene in his letter of the 22d of November, was so much hurt at it, that he takes particular pains to exculpate himself from any participation in that order. In this treatment, the militia shared the fate usually attending humble friends, who are seldom caressed by the great any longer than they can be subservient to their views or interests. Gen. Marion and his brigade were now to part forever. But as its movements had always been directed without pomp or parade, so its discharge was conducted with republican simplicity. In his favourite encampment at Watboo, and on the side of the cedar trees, he thanked his

Chapter 4: Campaign of 1782

officers and men for their many and useful services, and bid them a friendly and affectionate farewell. Two years and a half had now elapsed since Gen. Marion first assumed his command; his appearance was not prepossessing, his manners were distant, but not repulsive, yet few leaders have ever been so popular among their men; none ever had more of their confidence. He had so much influence as to settle amicably many disputes among his officers, and even private men; and never was a duel fought by any of them while under his immediate command. His stratagems appeared intuitive. Did Gen. Marion march in person to the attack?[4] then the common conclusion was, the enemy is taken by surprise, or we shall fight them on advantageous ground.

The revolutionary war raged no where more than it did where he commanded; in all this he had the head to lead and to plan, and the discernment to choose those who could best execute. His personal bravery was displayed on many occasions, but his own sword struck not the blow, it never was seen stained with blood; cool and collected, he was always the general, never the common soldier. In short the whole bent of his soul was how he should best provide for his men, how he could most annoy the enemy, and how he could soonest achieve the independence of his country. The characters of his officers will be best collected from the facts stated. In taking such wise measures as have been related for the defence of the lives and property of his friends, Gen. Marion could extend none of them to his own possessions. His plantation in St. John's lay within a mile of the marches and countermarches of the British, and was subject to every species of wanton waste and depredation. One half of his negroes were taken away, and the other half must have been faithful, or they would not have remained. He had ten workers left, but plantation utensils, clothes for his people, household furniture, and stock of cattle and horses, were all to be purchased without a cent of money.[5] He expected to receive half pay, but even in this was disappointed. At a session of the legislature shortly after, a garrison was established at fort Johnson, and he was appointed commander, with a salary of about 500 pounds.[6] Yet, in despite of his recent and meritorious services, this moderate appointment became a butt at which they who are forever seeking popularity by recommending curtailments in useful and even necessary expenditures, soon levelled their shafts. His spirit could not easily brook such treatment, but his debts made it prudent to submit.

At this juncture, his merit and high reputation had made a favourable impression on the heart of Miss Mary Videau, one of his relations. She was observed to be fond of hearing his achievements spoken of in terms of high approbation; some of the general's friends noticed it, and gave him a hint. He paid his addresses to her and was well received. They were soon after married, and he resigned his command at the fort. She brought him a handsome fortune, and as there was no great disparity, either in their years or disposition, she made him an excellent wife. She was in countenance the exact counterpart of the general. She partook in all his amusements, accompanied him in his journeys, and in his absence could not be better pleased than by hearing his praises. In short, nothing could have made this matrimonial connexion more happy, but its being more fruitful. They never had an heir. The general built a comfortable house of a single story, with one sitting room, but many chambers; its materials were of the most durable kind of cypress; but it received no coat either of paint or varnish. Here his friends were received with a hearty welcome and good cheer, and the stranger with kind hospitality. His planting interest was judiciously managed, and his property increased yearly. In the summer months he made excursions, into the upper country almost every year, for the benefit of his health. In these journeys he loved to renew former recollections. He had retained his marquee, camp bed and cooking utensils, and he always travelled as he had done in his brigade. To his wife nothing could be more pleasant, and she has often recounted these jaunts to her friends with delight. The old pot, kettle and frying-pan, tin plates, knives and forks were preserved as precious relics: the sumpter mules as friends. His faithful servant Oscar, who had accompanied him through all his difficulties, always received high marks of his favour. As to honours, Gen. Marion did not aspire higher than to a seat in the senate, which he continued to fill as long as he pleased, as a member for St. John's. In May, 1790, he was a member of the convention for forming the state constitution; after which he declined all public duties. In politics he was a moderate federalist; such as were many great revolutionary characters. In May, 1794, the militia of the state were re-organized, and soon after Gen. Marion resigned his commission in the militia. Shortly after his resignation, at a meeting of the citizens of Georgetown, a committee of four was appointed to draw up an address to the general. These were William D. James, Robert Brownfield, Thomas Mitchell and Joseph Blythe. An address was prepared by the chairman (James,) and unanimously adopted. Copies were also directed to be distributed through the district. It is as follows:

"Dear General,
At the present juncture, when the necessity of public affairs requires the military of this state to be organized anew, to repel the attacks of an enemy from whatever quarter they may be forced upon us, we, citizens of the district of Georgetown, finding you no longer at our head, have agreed to convey to you our grateful sentiments for your former numerous services. In the decline of life when the merits of the veteran are too often forgotten, we wish to remind you that yours are still fresh in the remembrance of your fellow citizens. Could it be possible for men who have served and fought under you, to be now forgetful of that general, by whose prudent conduct their lives have been saved and their families preserved from being plundered by a rapacious enemy? We mean not to flatter you. At this time it is impossible for you to

Chapter 4: Campaign of 1782

suspect it. Our present language is the language of free men expressing only sentiments of gratitude. Your achievements may not have sufficiently swelled the historic page. They were performed by those who could better wield the sword than the pen. By men whose constant dangers precluded them from the leisure, and whose necessities deprived them of the common implements of writing. But this is of little moment: they remain recorded in such indelible characters upon our minds, that neither change of circumstances nor length of time can efface them. Taught by us, our children shall hereafter point out the places and say to their children, here Gen. Marion, posted to advantage, made a glorious stand in defence of the liberties of his country; there, on disadvantageous ground, retreated to save the lives of his fellow citizens. What could be more glorious for the general commanding free men than thus to fight, and thus to save the lives of his fellow soldiers? Continue general in peace to till those acres which you once wrested from the hands of an enemy. Continue to enjoy dignity, accompanied with ease, and to lengthen out your days blessed with the consciousness of conduct unaccused of rapine or oppression, and of actions ever directed by the purest patriotism."

This address was presented to the general and gave him great pleasure; but as he had not latterly been much in the habit of using his pen, his answer was a verbal one, expressive of his sincere thanks.

On the 27th day of February, 1795, Gen. Marion died at his house in St. John's parish. As his fame is yet but indistinctly known, and much of that through the medium of fable, the present attempt has been made to arrest its progress, to do honour to his memory, and to transmit his example to posterity.

Gen. Marion's Epitaph.

Sacred to the Memory of BRIG. GEN. FRANCIS MARION, Who departed this life, on the 27th of February, 1795, In the Sixty-Third Year of his Age; Deeply regretted by all his fellow citizens.

HISTORY will record his worth, and rising generations embalm his memory, as one of the most distinguished Patriots and Heroes of the American Revolution; which elevated his native Country TO HONOUR AND INDEPENDENCE, and secured to her the blessings of LIBERTY AND PEACE.

This tribute of veneration and gratitude is erected in commemoration of the noble and disinterested virtues of the CITIZEN; and the gallant exploits of the SOLDIER; Who lived without fear, and died without reproach.

Taken from the marble slab at Belle Isle, this 20th September, 1821, by Theodore Gourdin.

Footnotes

1. Marion's letter to Horry, 10th January.
2. Count Rumford told professor Pictet, of Geneva, many years after, that he had never been able to efface from his imagination, the horrid spectacle of the dead and wounded upon these occasions.—See Pictet's Tour in England, p. 212.
3. Capt. Crafton's letter to Marion, 13th June, 1782.
4. Nil desperandum, Teucro duce.
5. Marion's letter to Col. P. Horry, 18th Jan. 1781.
6. Act, 10th March, 1784.

Appendix

The following is the letter of Dr. Robert Brownfield to the author, giving a detailed account of the defeat of Buford's regiment, referred to in Chapter II Paragraph 6.

Dear Sir,

In obedience to your request, I send you a detailed account of the defeat and massacre of Col. Buford's regiment, near the borders of North Carolina, on the road leading from Camden to Salisbury. This regiment consisting of three hundred and fifty men, well appointed and equipped, had marched from Virginia for the relief of Charleston, and had advanced to Santee, where they were met by intelligence of the surrender; a retreat then became unavoidable.—Between this place and Camden they fell in with Gen. Caswell, at the head of about seven hundred North Carolina militia, whose object had been the same, and whose retreat became equally imperious. At Camden these two corps unfortunately separated; Caswell filed off to Pedee, and Buford pursued the road to Salisbury. This measure was accounted for by the want of correct intelligence of Tarleton's prompt and rapid movements, who was in full pursuit with three hundred cavalry, and each a soldier of infantry behind him.— Neglecting Caswell and his militia, the pursuit was continued after Buford to the Waxhaw. Finding he was approximating this corps, he despatched a flag, saying he was at Barclay's with seven hundred men, and summoned them to surrender on the terms granted to the garrison in Charleston. Buford immediately laid the summons before a council of his officers with three distinct propositions from himself:—Shall we comply with Tarleton's summons? Shall we abandon the baggage, and, by a rapid movement, save ourselves? or, shall we fortify ourselves by the waggons, and wait his approach?

The first and second were decidedly rejected by the unanimous voice of the council, declaring it to be incompatible with their honour as soldiers, or the duty they owed their country, either to surrender or abandon the baggage on the bare statement of Tarleton. They had no certainty of the truth of his assertion, and that it might be only a ruse de guerre to alarm their fears and obtain a bloodless victory. The third was also negatived on the ground, that although they might by this means defend themselves against Tarleton, but as no succour was near, and as Tarleton could, in a short time, obtain reinforcements from Cornwallis, against which no effectual resistance could be made, this measure would be unavailable.

The discussion soon resulted in a resolution to continue the march, maintaining the best possible order for the reception of the enemy. In a short time Tarleton's bugle was heard, and a furious attack was made on the rear guard, commanded by Lieut. Pearson. Not a man escaped. Poor Pearson was inhumanely mangled on the face as he lay on his back. His nose and lip were bisected obliquely; several of his teeth were broken out in the upper jaw, and the under completely divided on each side. These wounds were inflicted after he had fallen, with several others on his head, shoulders, and arms. As a just tribute to the honour and Job-like patience of poor Pearson, it ought to be mentioned, that he lay for five weeks without uttering a single groan. His only nourishment was milk, drawn from a bottle through a quill. During that period he was totally deprived of speech, nor could he articulate distinctly after his wounds were healed.

This attack gave Buford the first confirmation of Tarleton's declaration by his flag. Unfortunately he was then compelled to prepare for action, on ground which presented no impediment to the full action of cavalry. Tarleton having arranged his infantry in the centre, and his cavalry on the wings, advanced to the charge with the horrid yells of infuriated demons. They were received with firmness, and completely checked, until the cavalry were gaining the rear. Buford now perceiving that further resistance was hopeless, ordered a flag to be hoisted and the arms to be grounded, expecting the usual treatment sanctioned by civilized warfare. This, however, made no part of Tarleton's creed. His ostensible pretext, for the relentless barbarity that ensued, was, that his horse was killed under him just as the flag was raised. He affected to believe that this was done afterwards, and imputed it to treachery on the part of Buford; but, in reality, a safe opportunity was presented to gratify that thirst for blood which marked his character in every conjuncture that promised probable impunity to himself. Ensign Cruit, who advanced with the flag, was instantly cut down. Viewing this as an earnest of what they were to expect, a resumption of their arms was attempted, to sell their lives as dearly as possible; but before this was fully effected, Tarleton with his cruel myrmidons was in the midst of them, when commenced a scene of indiscriminate carnage never surpassed by the ruthless atrocities of the most barbarous savages.

The demand for quarters, seldom refused to a vanquished foe, was at once found to be in vain;—not a man was spared—and it was the concurrent testimony of all the survivors, that for fifteen minutes after every man was prostrate. They went over the ground plunging their bayonets into every one that exhibited any signs of life, and in some instances, where several had fallen one over the other, these monsters were seen to throw off on the point of the bayonet the uppermost, to come at those beneath. Capt. Carter,[1] who

Appendix

commanded the artillery and who led the van, continued his march without bringing his guns into action; this conduct excited suspicions unfavourable to the character of Carter, and these were strengthened by his being paroled on the ground, and his whole company without insult or injury being made prisoners of war. Whether he was called to account for his conduct, I have never learnt. These excepted, the only survivors of this tragic scene were Capts. Stokes, Lawson and Hoard, Lieuts. Pearson and Jamison, and Ensign Cruit.

To consign to oblivion the memory of these gallant suffering few would be culpable injustice. When men have devoted their lives to the service of their country, and whose fate has been so singularly disastrous; there is an honest anxiety concerning them, springing from the best and warmest feelings of our nature, which certainly should be gratified. This is peculiarly the truth in regard to Capt. John Stokes, although in his military character perhaps not otherwise distinguished from his brother officers, than by the number of his wounds and the pre-eminence of sufferings. He received twenty-three wounds, and as he never for a moment lost his recollection, he often repeated to me the manner and order in which they were inflicted.

Early in the sanguinary conflict he was attacked by a dragoon, who aimed many deadly blows at his head, all of which by the dextrous use of the small sword he easily parried; when another on the right, by one stroke, cut off his right hand through the metacarpal bones. He was then assailed by both, and instinctively attempted to defend his head with his left arm until the forefinger was cut off, and the arm hacked in eight or ten places from the wrist to the shoulder. His head was then laid open almost the whole length of the crown to the eye brows. After he fell he received several cuts on the face and shoulders. A soldier passing on in the work of death, asked if he expected quarters? Stokes answered I have not, nor do I mean to ask quarters, finish me as soon as possible; he then transfixed him twice with his bayonet. Another asked the same question and received the same answer, and he also thrust his bayonet twice through his body. Stokes had his eye fixed on a wounded British officer, sitting at some distance, when a serjeant came up, who addressed him with apparent humanity, and offered him protection from further injury at the risk of his life. All I ask, said Stokes, is to be laid by that officer that I may die in his presence. While performing this generous office the humane serjeant was twice obliged to lay him down, and stand over him to defend him against the fury of his comrades. Doct. Stapleton, Tarleton's surgeon, whose name ought to be held up to eternal obloquy, was then dressing the wounds of the officer. Stokes, who lay bleeding at every pore, asked him to do something for his wounds, which he scornfully and inhumanely refused, until peremptorily ordered by the more humane officer, and even then only filled the wounds with rough tow, the particles of which could not be separated from the brain for several days.

Capt. Stokes was a native of Pittsylvania county, Virginia. He was early intended for the bar, and having gone through the usual course of classical and other preparatory studies, he commenced the practice with the most flattering indications of future eminence. But the calm pursuits of peace not comporting with the ardour of his mind, he relinquished the fair prospect of professional emolument, and accepted a captaincy in Buford's regiment.

At this catastrophe, he was about twenty-seven years of age. His height was about the common standard; his figure and appearance, even in his mangled situation, inspired respect and veneration; and the fire of genius that sparkled in his dark piercing eye, gave indications of a mind fitted not only for the field, but for all the departments of civil life.

Shortly after the adoption of the constitution of the United States, he was promoted to the bench in the Federal Court—married Miss Pearson—and settled on the Yadkin river, where the county is called Stokes, after his name.

(Signed,)
R. Brownfield.

* * * * *

The following letter from Major Keating Simons, was received too late to be inserted either in the body, or in a note to this work, although it contains one of the finest traits of the character of Gen. Marion.—Major Muller and Major Simons acted as brigade majors to the general, and both were high in his confidence.

After the war Major Simons engaged in the useful business of a factor, and received the patronage and approbation of numerous friends. While himself labouring under many difficulties, arising from the war, he extended his helping hand to his old friend the general, struggling from the same cause under still greater embarrassments, and had the satisfaction to assist in extricating him from many of them. This debt of gratitude was not forgotten; when Mrs. Marion was dying she left the one half of her fortune to the late Keating Lewis Simons, Esq. eldest son of the major: but two short years since the ornament of the bar and of his country.

Charleston, November 17th, 1821.
Dear Sir,
The anecdote of Gen. Marion you requested me to relate to you, I now take the first opportunity to mention. It occurred late in the year 1782, when the British troops were preparing to evacuate Charleston: they had a covering party on James' island to protect their wood-cutters, and another on Lamprere's point to protect their getting water for their shipping. Col. Kosciusko, a Polander, solicited Gen. Greene to afford him an opportunity of distinguishing himself;

Appendix

and as the covering party to the wood-cutters was the only one which now presented itself, the general gave him a command to attack them, which he did, and was defeated with the loss of a great many men, and among the slain was the gallant Capt. Wilmot.

About the same time that Gen. Greene gave Kosciusko this command, he wrote to Gen. Marion, "that he understood the watering party at Lamprere's point was so situated as to afford him an opportunity of attacking it with success." Gen. Marion replied, "that he had not overlooked the situation of the British at that spot, but he viewed the war in Carolina as over, and as the enemy were preparing to go away, he had sent a party to protect them from being annoyed by his own men; that he commanded his fellow citizens who had already shed blood enough in the cause of freedom, and that he would not spill another drop of it, now when it was unnecessary; no, not for the highest honours that could be conferred upon him."

If you think this anecdote worth mentioning in the biography of that great man, it is quite at your service.

With much respect and esteem,

I am, dear Sir,

Yours very truly,

Keating Simons.

Correspondence.

Gen. Lincoln to Lieut. Col. Marion, at Sheldon.

Head Quarters, Charleston, Jan. 31, 1780.

Sir,

The state of affairs is such as to make it necessary that we draw our force to a point as much and as soon as possible. No troops will be kept in the field except two hundred light infantry and the horse.* You will, therefore, please to select from the three regiments with you, two hundred of your best men, and those who are best clothed, and organize them into corps with proper officers. All the remainder with the baggage of the whole (saving such as is absolutely necessary for light troops) will march immediately to this town. You will please take the command of the light infantry, until Lieut. Col. Henderson arrives, which I expect will be in a few days. After that I wish to see you as soon as possible in Charleston.—Cross will deliver you this with a letter to Col. Parker, and another to Major Jamieson. You will send them towards Augusta in the common route by four horsemen. Two will guide Col. Parker to this town by the shortest way, the other two will guide Major Jamieson to your camp.

Washington's.

I am, Sir,

Your most obedient servant,

B. Lincoln.

* * * * *

Col. Marion to Col. P. Horry.
Lynch's Creek, Aug. 17, 1780.[2]
Sir,
You will take the command of such men as will be collected from Capts. Bounneau's, Mitchell's and Benson's companies, and immediately proceed to Santee, from the lower ferry to Lenud's, and destroy all the boats and canoes on the river, and post guards at each crossing place, to prevent persons from crossing to or from Charleston, on either side of the river.—You will give all necessary intelligence, and the number of men you may have collected as early as possible. You will procure about twenty-five weight of gunpowder, and a proportionable quantity of ball or swanshot, also flints, and send them up to me immediately, to the Kingstree, by an express.

I am with esteem,
Your obedient servant,
Francis Marion.
N. B.—You will also take the command of Capt. Lenud's company, and furnish your men with arms, wherever you can find them, giving receipts.

* * * * *

Extract of a Letter from Col. Marion to Col. P. Horry.
Lynch's Creek, Aug. 27, 1780.
Dear Sir,
I am sorry to acquaint you that Gen. Gates is defeated with great loss; he was obliged to retreat to Charlotte, which obliges me also to retreat. You will without delay retreat with what men you can get, to Briton's neck, where I have encamped. It is necessary to obtain ammunition, arms and accoutrements, and as many horses as you can get; also stores from Georgetown, which you will send if possible up the river to Briton's neck.

On the 20th inst. I attacked a guard of the 63d and Prince of Wales' regiment, with a number of tories, at the Great Savannah, near Nelson's ferry. Killed and took twenty-two regulars, and two tories prisoners, and retook one hundred and fifty continentals of the Maryland line; one waggon and a drum; one captain and a subaltern were also captured. Our loss is one killed, and Capt. Benson is slightly wounded on the head.

* * * * *

Appendix

Brig. Gen. Marion to Adjt. Postell.[3]
Snow's Island, Dec. 30, 1780.
Sir,

You will proceed with a party down Black river, from Black Mingo to the mouth of Pedee, and come up to this place; you will take all the boats and canoes from Euhaney up, and impress negroes to bring them to camp; put some men to see them safe; you will take every horse, to whomsoever he may belong, whether friend or foe. You will take all arms and ammunition for the use of our service. You will forbid all persons from carrying any grains, stock or any sort of provisions to Georgetown, or where the enemy may get them, on pain of being held as traitors and enemies to the Americans. All persons who will not join you you will take prisoners and bring to me. You will return as soon as possible. Let me know any intelligence you may gain of the enemy's strength or movements.

I am, your obedient servant,
Francis Marion.
Adjt. Postell.
N. B.—You will bring up as much rice and salt in the boats as possible.

* * * * *

Gen. Marion to Capt. John Postell.
Goddard's Plantation,[4] Pedee, Jan. 19, 1781.
Dear Sir,

I send Lieut. King with fifteen men, to reinforce you. I would have all the flats and boats you can collect, loaded with rice, and sent to Mr. Joseph Allston's plantation, on Bull's creek, to the north of Pedee, where there is a ferry to Euhaney; and the rice is to be there stored, and the boats kept going until all that is beat out in your district is carried. From there I will send for it up higher. You must take such negroes for the boats as belong to those persons who may be with the enemy, or from those estates which the enemy think forfeited. Gen. Greene is in want of a number of negroes—say fifty—for the use of the army. You will collect them in your district, and send them to me; taking care not to distress any family, but taking them where they can be best spared. I shall detain those negroes that came up with the boats you have sent. One boat has arrived, and I have sent to assist in getting up the others. I beg you would give me intelligence of the movements of the enemy in Georgetown, and, if possible, their particular strength: what corps of horse and foot, and how many militia, and if there are any cannon mounted on their redoubt, and whether they are making any new works. You will send Capt. W——, and Mr. S——, and all such men (who have taken, or are suspected of having taken part with the enemy) to me. You must not suffer any person to carry property where the enemy has possession, or have any intercourse with them.

I am, with regard, dear Sir,
Your obedient servant,
Francis Marion.

* * * * *

Extract of a Letter from Gen. Marion to Capt. Postell.
January 19, 1781.
Dear Sir,
Your father may keep the canoe you mention. I have received the prisoners, by Mr. M'Pherson,[5] and shall give them the pleasure of seeing head quarters.

I am, dear Sir,
Your obedient servant,
Francis Marion.

* * * * *

Gen. Greene to Gen. Marion.
Camp, on Pedee, Jan. 19, 1781.
Dear Sir,
The enclosed letter, from Capt. Odingsells, came to hand last evening, I have directed him to apply to you for orders on the subject. I have detached Major Anderson, with one thousand regulars, and one hundred Virginia militia, to attack and disperse the tories at Mr. Amy's mill, on Drowning creek. The party marched yesterday, with orders to endeavour to surprise them; perhaps you might be able to make some detachment that would contribute to their success. By the last accounts, Lieut. Col. Tarleton was in motion, with about one thousand troops, towards Gen. Morgan, who is in the fork of Broad river. Lord Cornwallis is moving in force to cover him. I wish your answer respecting the practicability of surprising the party near Nelson's; the route, and force you will be able to detach. This inquiry is a matter that requires the greatest secrecy.

I am, dear Sir,
Your most obedient humble servant,
N. Greene.

* * * * *

Appendix

Gen. Greene to Gen. Marion.
Camp,[6] Jan. 22, 1781.
Sir,

I have received your letter of the 18th, containing an account of the several little skirmishes between your people and the enemy, which were clever and do them much honour. I am sorry that so few horses fit for service are to be had in your quarter, as we are in great want. Get as many as you can, and let us have fifteen or twenty sent to camp without loss of time, they being wanted for immediate service. Major Hyrne who is appointed deputy commissary general of prisoners, has settled the business with Mr. Walter. I beg you will please to favour me with weekly returns of the militia serving under you, and the number of horses you have in service, and the particular duties on which they are employed, to be made every Monday morning. I also wish separate returns of the continental troops serving with you, the rank and names of the officers, and the corps to which they belong.

I am, Sir, Your most obedient servant, N. Greene.

* * * * *

Brig. Gen. Marion to Capt. John Postell.
January 23, 1781.
Sir,

Particular circumstances make me desire that you will immediately march all the men under your command to join me at the Kingstree; you must proceed by forced marches until you come up to me, for no time is to be lost. Leave your post as secretly as possible, without letting any one know where you are going, or of your intention to leave it.

I am, Sir, Your obedient servant, Francis Marion.

* * * * *

Gen. Greene to Gen. Marion.
Camp, on Pedee, Jan. 23, 1781.
Dear Sir,

I have the particular pleasure to congratulate you on the entire defeat of the enemy under Lieut. Col. Tarleton. Major Giles, this moment arrived, brings the glorious intelligence, which I have the pleasure to transmit.

On the 17th, at day-break, the enemy consisting of eleven hundred and fifty British troops, and fifty militia, attacked Gen. Morgan, who was at the Cowpens, between Pacolet and Broad river, with two hundred and ninety infantry, eighty cavalry and about six hundred militia. The action lasted fifty minutes and was remarkably severe. Our brave troops charged the enemy with bayonets, and entirely routed them, killing near one hundred and fifty, wounding upwards of two hundred, and taking more than five hundred prisoners, exclusive of the prisoners with two pieces of artillery, thirty-five waggons, upwards of one hundred dragoon horses, and with the loss only of ten men killed and fifty-five wounded. Our intrepid party pursued the enemy upwards of twenty miles. About thirty commissioned officers are among the prisoners. Col. Tarleton had his horse killed and was wounded, but made his escape with two hundred of his troops. This important intelligence I wish you to communicate to Lieut. Col. Lee if possible. I have not time to write him. If he has not attacked Georgetown, I wish he could privately transmit it to the garrison.

I am with esteem, Your most obedient humble servant, N. Greene.

* * * * *

Extract of a Letter from Gen. Greene to Gen. Marion.
 Camp, on Pedee, Jan. 25, 1781.
Dear Sir,
Your letter of the 20th is before me; before this I hope you have received the agreeable news of the defeat of Lieut. Col. Tarleton by Gen. Morgan; after this nothing will appear difficult.

* * * * *

Gen. Huger to Brig. Gen. Marion.
 Camp, Hick's Creek, Jan. 28, 1781.
Dear Sir,
Gen. Greene wishes that you will attempt to cross the Santee, and if possible reach some of the enemy's magazines and destroy them. I am persuaded you will not leave any practicable measure unattempted to effect this business. The execution is left entirely to your judgment and address.

I am, dear Sir, With much esteem, Your most obedient humble servant, Is. Huger.

* * * * *

Gen. Marion to Capt. John Postell.
 Cordes' Plantation, Jan. 29, 1781.
Dear Sir,
You will cross Santee river with twenty-five men, and make a forced march to Watboo bridge, there burn all the British stores of every kind; it is possible you will find a small guard there, which you may surprise, but bring no prisoners with you. You will return the same way, and recross the river

Appendix

at the same place, which must be done before daylight next morning. After effecting my purpose at Watboo, it will not be out of your way to come by Monk's corner, and destroy any stores or waggons you may find there. You can learn from the people at Watboo what guard there is at the corner; if it should be too strong you will not attempt that place. In going to Watboo, you must see if there is a guard at the church; if there is you will shun it; you will consider provisions of all kinds British property. The destruction of all the British stores in the above-mentioned places is of the greatest consequence to us, and only requires boldness and expedition. Take care that your men do not get at liquor, or clog themselves with plunder so as to endanger their retreat.

I am with regard, dear Sir, Your obedient servant, Francis Marion.

* * * * *

Gen. Greene to Gen. Marion.
Camp, at Guilford Court House, Feb. 11, 1781.
Dear Sir,

I received your favour of the 31st ult. and request you to give my particular thanks to Major and Capt. Postell for the spirit and address with which they executed your orders over the Santee. Your crossing the Santee must depend upon your own discretion. I think it would be attended with many advantages, if it can be executed with safety. Gen. Sumter is desired to call out all the militia of South Carolina and employ them in destroying the enemy's stores and perplexing their affairs in the state. Please to communicate and concert with him your future operations until we have a better opportunity to have more free intercourse. Great activity is necessary to keep the spirits of the people from sinking, as well as to alarm the enemy respecting the safety of their posts. We formed a junction at this place last night, but our force is so much inferior to the enemy's that we dare not hazard a general action if it can be avoided, but I am not certain that it can. The enemy are within thirty miles of us, up towards the shallow ford on the Yadkin.

I am, dear Sir, Your most obedient humble servant, N. Greene.

* * * * *

Gen. Greene to Gen. Marion.
Camp, at Halifax Court House, Virginia, Feb. 16, 1781.
Dear Sir,

I have seen your letter to Gen. Huger of the 6th inst. and am surprised that Col. Baker or Capt. Snipes should pretend that they had my directions for crossing the Santee. I beg you will encourage the militia and engage them to continue their exertions.—If the supplies expected from the northward arrive in season, we shall be able to assist you. The movements of the enemy were so rapid, that few of the militia joined us on our march from Pedee, which reduced us to the necessity of passing the Dan, or risking an action on very unequal terms. The enemy are upon the banks of the river, but the people of this country appear to be in earnest. I hope we shall soon be able to push Lord Cornwallis in turn. I wrote to you from Guilford, which I hope you have received.

I am, dear Sir, Your most obedient servant,
N. Greene.

* * * * *

Gen. Marion to Lieut. Col. Balfour.
 Santee, March 7, 1781.
 Sir,

I sent Capt. John Postell with a flag to exchange some prisoners, which Capt. Saunders, commandant of Georgetown, had agreed to, but contrary to the law of nations, he has been seized and detained as a prisoner. As I cannot imagine that his conduct will be approved of by you, I hope orders will be immediately given to have my flag discharged, or I must immediately acquaint congress of this violation. The ill consequence of which it is now in your power to prevent. I am sorry to complain of the ill treatment my officers and men meet with from Capt. Saunders; the officers are closely employed in a small place, where they can neither stand or lie at length, nor have they more than half rations. I have treated your officers and men who have fallen into my hands in a different manner. Should these evils not be prevented in future, it will not be in my power to prevent retaliation. Lord Rawdon and Col. Watson have hanged three men of my brigade for supposed crimes, which will make as many of your men in my hands suffer. I hope this will be prevented in future, for it is my wish to act with humanity and tenderness to those unfortunate men, the chances of war may throw in my power.

I have the honour to be Your obedient servant, Francis Marion.

* * * * *

Gen. Marion to Col. Watson, of the British.
 Santee, March 7, 1781.
 Sir,

Enclosed is a letter which I wish may be forwarded as soon as possible. I make no doubt but that you will be surprised to see a flag sent at the head of an armed party. The reason of it is, that Capt. Saunders, commandant of Georgetown, has violated the law of nations, by taking, detaining and imprisoning Capt. Postell, who carried prisoners to exchange, which was agreed to by him. The hanging of prisoners and the violation of my flag will be retaliated if a stop is not put to such proceedings, which are disgraceful to all civilized nations. All of your officers and men who have fallen into my hands, have been treated with humanity and tenderness; and I wish sincerely that I may not be obliged to act contrary to my inclinations; but such treatment as my unhappy followers, whom the chances of war may throw in the hands of my enemies receive, such may those expect who fall in my hands.

I have the honour to be Your obedient servant, Francis Marion.

* * * * *

Extract of a Letter from Gov. J. Rutledge to Gen. Marion.
Camp, at Haw River, March 8, 1781.
I have not yet received the blank militia commissions I expected out. If I do not get some before I arrive at Richmond, I will there have some printed and transmitted to you. In the mean time you will give brevets, and in order that you may carry sufficient authority over the several officers in your brigade, you may remove any of them, and appoint others in their stead, from time to time, as you think proper.

* * * * *

Col. N. Balfour to Brig. Gen. Marion.
Charleston, March 12, 1781.
Sir,
I have received your letter of the 7th inst. respecting the detention of Capt. John Postell, when charged with a flag of truce to Georgetown, and complaining of the same as a breach of the law of nations. The best answer I can return to which is the transmission of his parole, which will clearly evince that the breach of such law, as well as those of honour, rest solely with that gentleman, who has acted in a military capacity when engaged by the most solemn ties to remain in a state of neutrality.

* * * * *

Col. Balfour to Gen. Marion.
Charleston, March 21, 1781.
Sir,
I am greatly astonished to find that you have detained one of our officers,[7] sent out with a flag of truce to you, and acting under its sanction; this is indeed an infraction of the laws of nations and of war, as you complain of in the case of Capt. Postell, and such a one as if not immediately redressed I shall be

obliged to punish in the most exemplary manner by the severest retaliation. If in this action you could have alluded to the case of Capt. Postell, my letter of the 12th inst. must surely have convinced you, how truly dissimilar they are in every respect; but as from such conduct I must conceive, Sir, this letter may not have reached you, I now enclose a copy for your information and conviction. Let me observe, as faith had been violated by Capt. Postell, he naturally became to us an object for capture and punishment, under whatsoever circumstances he might be met, and to argue from his justifiable detention, a right to extend the like to those most unimpeachably upright in their conduct, is a confounding of right and wrong, and a violation of all principles under which any intercourse can subsist between powers at war with each other.

I am, Sir, Your most obedient humble servant, N. Balfour.

* * * * *

Col. Watson to Gen. Marion.
Blakely's, March 15, 1781.
Sir,
The very extraordinary method you took of sending the letter I received from you, makes it rather difficult to guess in what way you mean to carry on this war, and therefore induces me to take the mode of addressing you through a neutral person. The bearer is a little boy of John Witherspoon's. We have an officer and some men wounded, whom I should be glad to send where they could be better taken care of. I wish therefore to know if they will be permitted to pass, without interruption from any of your parties, to Charleston.

Yours, &c. (Signed) John Watson.

P.S.—If you have no objection to their going, you will be so good as to send a pass for them.

* * * * *

Col. Watson to Gen. Marion.
Blakely's, March 16, 1781.
Sir,
I do not think it necessary to enter into a detail of your conduct, or by words to justify our own. Your mentioning that you wished to carry on the war as usual with civilized nations, led me to mention the circumstance I did. Care is taken to prevent any thing being taken from those who do not bear arms against us, or who do not directly assist our enemies; whatever other people are deprived of we do not call plunder, but property fairly taken from the enemy; and what cannot be carried away conveniently we destroy, if we think proper. The burning of houses and the property of the inhabitants, who

Appendix

are our enemies, is customary in all civilized nations. But further than the distress that is occasioned to their families, the distressing women and children, is so far from being countenanced by any officers in our service, that on the contrary every assistance possible is afforded them.

I am, Sir, Yours, &c. (Signed) John Watson.

* * * * *

Capt. John Saunders to Gen. Marion.
Georgetown, March 24, 1781.
Sir,

The enclosed were received from Lieut. Col. Balfour, with orders to forward them to you. There is such an apparent dissimilarity in the cases of Mr. Merritt and Mr. Postell, that I am confident that Mr. Merritt will be immediately sent in. I am happy to hear by Capt. Spencer, who fell into my hands yesterday, that the detention of Mr. Merritt is occasioned equally by that act as by sending an improper person with a flag.

I am, Sir, Yours, &c. (Signed) John Saunders, Commandant, Georgetown.

* * * * *

Gen. Greene to Gen. Marion.
Camp, Deep River, April 4, 1781.
Dear Sir,

This will be handed to you by Capt. Conyers,[8] who will inform you what we have contemplated. He is sent forward to collect provisions for the subsistence of the army, and I beg you will assist him in this necessary business. The army will march tomorrow, and I hope you will be prepared to support its operations with a considerable force; Gen. Sumter is written to, and I doubt not will be prepared to cooperate with us. The captain can give you a full history of Lord Cornwallis' manoeuvers in this state, and of the several skirmishes as well as the battle of Guilford, which finally terminated in a retreat of the enemy, and his lordship was obliged in turn to run hastily.

I am, dear Sir, yours, &c. N. Greene.

* * * * *

Gen. Greene to Gen. Marion.

Head Quarters, Widow Shoemaker's, April 17, 1781.

Dear Sir,

We are on our march for Camden, and shall be there the day after tomorrow. I am greatly in the dark respecting the enemy's strength and situation in South Carolina, and also of Lord Cornwallis' motions. This last circumstance is of the highest importance to the safety of our army, and I beg you to communicate to me all the intelligence you can obtain, and take measures to get all you can. Lieut. Col. Lee is gone towards the Santee; intelligence to him is as equally necessary as to me. You will please therefore to send him information accordingly. Do not spare either time or pains, and forward it as soon as possible. Your present force and situation I should be glad to have a particular account of. Please give me an official account of Col. Horry's attack upon a party of Watson's detachment.

I am, dear Sir, Yours, &c. (Signed) N. Greene.

* * * * *

Extract of a Letter from Col. Harden to Gen. Marion.

Camp, on Saltketcher, April 17, 1781.

Dear General,

I marched on, and got within sight of Fort Balfour, at Pocotaligo, at twelve o'clock in the day; I placed my men, and sent ten of the best horses to draw them out, but luckily Cols. Fenwick and Letchmere were at Vanberst, and were taken with seven of the dragoons, and brought to me; the rest were in the fort. I then sent Capt. Harden with a flag, to demand a surrender of the fort and the men in it; they sent for answer, they would not give it up. I sent the second time, and told them that if I was obliged to storm the fort, that I would give no quarter. Col. Kelsel then desired half an hour to consider. I gave him twenty minutes: they then agreed to give up the fort on terms which I granted; and in two hours, the fort with one militia colonel, one major, three captains, three lieutenants and sixty privates of Col. Fenwick's, one lieutenant and twenty-two dragoons with their horses, gave up to me, and they marched out and piled their arms without the abbatis; and I marched in and took possession of it; and during that night and the next day had it destroyed.

(Signed) Wm. Harden.

* * * * *

Appendix

Gen. Marion to Gen. Greene.
Fort Watson, (Scott's Lake) April 23, 1781.
Sir,

Lieut. Col. Lee made a junction with me at Santee, the 14th inst. after a rapid march from Ramsay's mill, on Deep river, which he performed in eight days. The 15th we marched to this place and invested it. Our hope was to cut off their water. Some riflemen and continentals immediately took post between the fort and the lake. The fort is situated on a small hill, forty feet high, stockaded, and with three rows of abbatis around it. No trees near enough to cover our men from their fire. The third day after we had invested it, we found the enemy had sunk a well near the stockade, which we could not prevent them from; as we had no entrenching tools to make our approach, we immediately determined to erect a work equal in height to the fort. This arduous work was completed this morning by Major Maham, who undertook it. We then made a lodgment on the side of the mount near the stockade. This was performed with great spirit and address by Ensign Johnson and Mr. Lee, a volunteer in Col. Lee's legion, who with difficulty ascended the hill and pulled away the abbatis, which induced the commandant to hoist a flag; and Col. Lee and myself agreed to the enclosed capitulation, which I hope may be approved of by you. Our loss on this occasion is two killed, and three continentals and three militia wounded. I am particularly indebted to Col. Lee for his advice and indefatigable diligence in every part of these tedious operations, against as strong a little post as could be well made, and on the most advantageous spot that could be wished for. The officers and men of the legion and militia, performed every thing that could be expected, and Major Maham, of my brigade, had, in a particular manner, a great share of this success, by his unwearied diligence, in erecting a tower which principally occasioned the reduction of the fort. In short, Sir, I have had the greatest assistance from every one under my command. Enclosed is a list of the prisoners and stores taken, and I shall, without loss of time, proceed to demolish the fort; after which I shall march to the High Hills of Santee, encamp at Capt. Richardson's, and await your orders.

(Signed) Francis Marion.

* * * * *

Extract of a Letter from Gen. Greene to Gen. Marion.
Camp, before Camden, April 24, 1781.
Dear Sir,

I thank you for the measures you have taken to furnish us with provisions, and for the intelligence you communicate. A field piece is coming to your assistance, which I hope will enable you and Col. Lee to get possession of the fort. With the artillery you will receive one hundred pounds of powder and four hundred pounds of lead; I wish my present stock would enable me to forward you a larger supply, but it will not, having sent you nearly half we have.

(Signed) N. Greene.

* * * * *

Gen. Greene to Gen. Marion.
Head Quarters, before Camden, April 26, 1781.
Dear Sir,

I have to acknowledge the receipt of your two letters, dated 23d and 25th inst. I congratulate you on your success against Fort Watson. The articles of capitulation I highly approve of, and feel myself particularly indebted to you, and all the officers and men under you, for their spirit, perseverance and good conduct upon the occasion. The enemy advanced upon us yesterday and gave us battle. The conflict was short, and seemed at one time to promise us advantage; but we were obliged to retire and give up the field; though without material loss. We are now within five miles of Camden, and shall closely invest it in a day or two again. That we may be enabled to operate with more certainty against this post, I should be glad you would move up immediately to our assistance, and take post on the north side of the town. I have detached a field piece to your assistance, with an escort of a few continental troops under the command of Major Eaton. I should be glad you would send them a guide and conduct them to your camp.

I am, Sir, With great esteem and respect, Yours, &c. (Signed) N. Greene.
P.S.—I should be glad you would move up within seven miles of Camden.

* * * * *

Gen. Greene to Gen. Marion.
Camp, at Cornal's Creek, May 9, 1781.
Dear Sir,

I am favoured with yours of the 6th instant. I am sorry the militia are deserting,[9] because there is no greater support. If they were influenced by proper principles, and were impressed with a love of liberty and a dread of slavery, they would not shrink at difficulties. If we had a force sufficient to recover the country, their aid would not be wanted, and they cannot be well acquainted with their true interest to desert us, because they conceive our force unequal to the reduction of the country without their consent. I shall be always happy to see you at head quarters, but cannot think you seriously mean to solicit leave to go to Philadelphia. It is true your task has been disagreeable, but not more so than others. It is now going on seven years since the commencement of this war. I have never had leave of absence an hour, nor paid the least attention to my own private affairs. Your state is invaded; your all is at stake; what has been done will signify nothing unless we persevere to the end. I left a wife in distress and every thing dear and valuable, to come and afford you all the assistance in my power, and if you leave us in the midst of our difficulties, while you have it so much in your power to promote the service, it must throw a damp upon the spirits of the army, to find that the first men in the state are retiring from the busy service, to indulge themselves in more agreeable amusements. However, your reasons for wishing to decline the command of the militia, may be more pressing than I imagine. I will therefore, add nothing more upon this subject till I see you. My reasons for writing so pressingly respecting the dragoons, was from the distress we were in. It is not my wish to take the horses from the militia if it will injure the public service—the effects and consequences you can better judge of than I can. You have rendered important service to the public with the militia under your command, and done great honour to yourself; and I would not wish to render your situation less agreeable with them, unless it is to answer some very great purpose; and this I persuade myself you would agree to from a desire to promote the public good. I wish you success in the fort you are besieging. Lord Rawdon was out yesterday; we had the night before taken a new position on Sawney's creek, and I imagine he came out to attack, expecting to find us on the Twenty-five mile creek. We did not like the position on Sawney's creek to risk an action on, and therefore took a new one at this place, leaving the horse, light infantry and picketts at the old encampment; the enemy came and drew up on the other side of the creek, but did not attempt to cross, and retired into Camden before night. We are in daily expectation of a large reinforcement of Virginia militia and some continental troops; when those arrive we shall push our operations with more vigour. No further news of Lord Cornwallis.

I am, Sir, With the highest esteem and regard, Yours, &c. N. Greene.

* * * * *

Gen. Greene to Gen. Marion.
Camp, before Ninety-Six, June 10, 1781.
Dear Sir,

I have to acknowledge the receipt of your favours of the 22d and 29th ult. It gives me great pleasure to hear the enemy have left Georgetown, and I am of opinion with you, that it will be attended with many good consequences to that part of the country. After you have dismantled the enemy's works, you will collect your force, take the position you mentioned, and act in conjunction with Gen. Sumter, agreeable to the advice I gave you before. I have the pleasure to congratulate you on the reduction of the enemy's fort at Augusta. This event took place on the 7th inst. by capitulation; and I hope in a few days to have the pleasure of congratulating you on the reduction of this place; but we are opposed to many difficulties, and the garrison resists with great obduracy.

I am, Sir, With every sentiment of respect and esteem, Yours, &c. N. Greene.

* * * * *

Extract of a Letter from Gen. Greene to Gen. Marion.
Head Quarters, near Sandy River, June 25, 1781.
Dear Sir,

I am favoured with your letter dated at the Congaree. The enemy have obliged us to raise the siege of Ninety-Six, when it was upon the eve of surrendering. It was my wish to have fought Lord Rawdon before he reached Ninety-Six, and could I have collected your force and that of Gen. Sumter and Pickens, I would have done it: and am persuaded we should have defeated him; but being left alone, I was obliged to retire.

(Signed) N. Greene.

Footnotes

1. Not Capt. Benjamin Carter, of Camden.
2. Written about a week after Gen. Marion took command of the militia.
3. Major John Postell.
4. Snow's Island.
5. Depeyster's company of grenadiers.
6. Camp Hicks.
7. Capt. Merritt.
8. Soon after Major Conyers.
9. This letter is an answer to one of Marion's, (which is missing,) soon after his arrival at Fort Watson, with only eighty men. See Chapter 3 Paragraph 26.

Printed in Great Britain
by Amazon